Dare to Daniel

Jenny Noon

Copyright © 2023 *Jenny Noon*

All Rights Reserved

In memory of Mum.
Dedicated to Dad and the Kingsway Kids.

Contents

About The Author ....

Introduction i

Chapter 1: Daniel and Maud, and Where it all Began. 1

Chapter 2: Off the Rails .... 1.

Chapter 3: The Homestead 19

Chapter 4: A Converted Railway Carriage 2:

Chapter 5: Noonies' Ten Thousand Kids 3

Chapter 6: Neighbours and Careers 4

Chapter 7: Denis Noon's Story 5

Chapter 8: 1945 – Denis' War Begins 6

Chapter 9: Service in the Middle East 7

Chapter 10: The Conversion 8

Chapter 11: Fishing For Souls 9

Chapter 12: Prizes and Surprises 9

Chapter 13: The Yorkshire Sunday School Camp 10

Chapter 14: Take it as Gospel - Building a New Gospel Hall. 11

Chapter 15: Daytrips and Jaunts 11

Chapter 16: God's Great Commission 13

Chapter 17: Defending the Faith 14

Chapter 18: The End of the Line. 152

Chapter 19: Denis Retires 156

Chapter 20: The Last Stop 165

Acknowledgements... 169

About The Author

Jenny Noon lives in North London with her husband Richard, rescue dog Nancy and some ex-battery hens. She worked for over 30 years in magazine publishing and her retirement coincided with the start of the Covid 19 lockdown. With her two daughters away at University, she has plenty of free time to do the things she loves. This includes writing this story, country walks, as well as volunteering on local gardening projects. Perhaps most proudly she holds a job of 'high office' as letting secretary for the local allotments.

Introduction

At the end of dinner in *Rules* (a Covent Garden institution and London's oldest restaurant), I ordered the cheese course – the Stilton cheese course, to be precise. A short while later, and somewhat unexpectedly, a whole Stilton arrived. I confess I had never seen a whole one before. But this Stilton was enormous, about a foot in diameter, and accompanied by the most unlikely and ridiculous of cheese-eating implements – a teaspoon! It had to be patiently pointed out to me to use the spoon to scoop out a small portion from the whole and pass the terrifying truckle to the next person to do the same.

At the same time though, I realised that I had finally understood something I had been taught years earlier in a training course, but I confess had never quite grasped. In simple terms, it is this: it is impossible to eat a whole Stilton at one sitting. The very thought of biting into the claggy, acidic, soapy texture is enough to start the gagging reflex, but crumble a few morsels on the top of a Waldorf salad, and you will discover an exquisite taste sensation that is effortless to digest. This life lesson, comprehensively illustrated before me in that famous old restaurant, is that when a task seems too big, break off a little piece at a time, and you'll find the exercise can be comfortably completed.

This is exactly how I felt about writing my dad, Denis' life story. I knew I wanted to do it, but the task seemed insurmountable, and I had put it off for years. Coincidentally, my grandfather, Daniel's story started exactly 100 years ago. His son, my Dad, is now ninety-five years old and Mum, whose memory was always to be relied upon, passed away this year aged ninety-three. I've always known that the life my parents and grandparents lived is interesting and unique. My friends used to clamour for tales of their 'unusual' antics. Their story is also pegged to the moment when a change in religious sentiment evolved into a new religious movement which my family committed to with unwavering resolve.

So, having whet readers' appetites, it's time to pick up the teaspoon and break off that first piece of Stilton.

JENNY NOON

November 2022

London

Dare to be a Daniel

Dare to be a Daniel

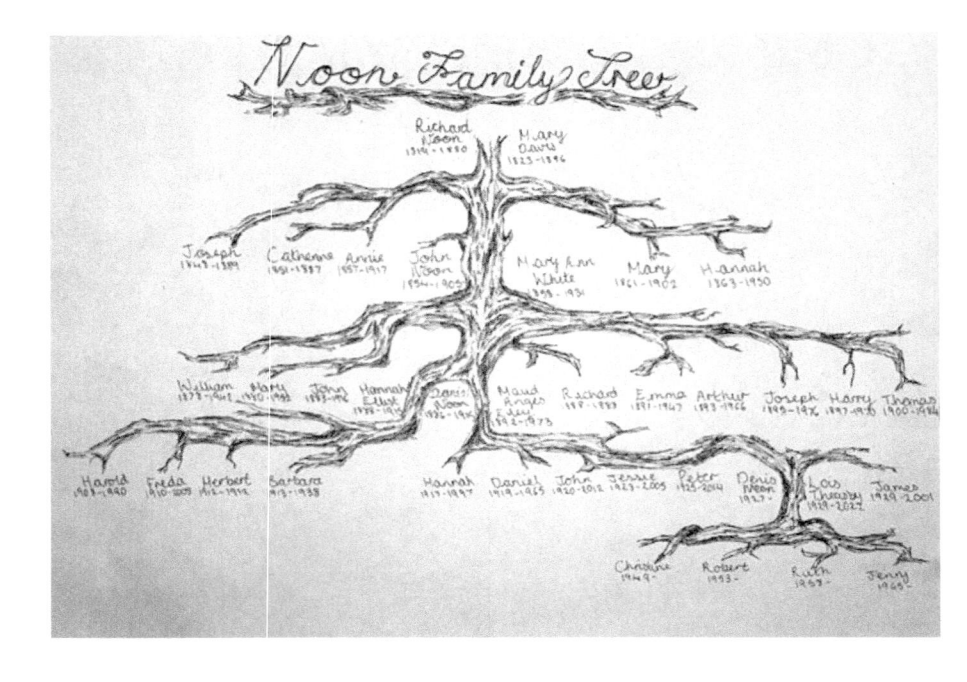

Chapter 1: Daniel and Maud, and Where it all Began.

This story starts at the turn of the 19th century in a suburb of the small town of Castleford in the North of England. Called Glasshoughton, it sits within the county of West Yorkshire and borders Castleford's sister town, Pontefract.

With a population of 50,000, Castleford is widely known for its factory outlet and entertainment mecca Junction 32, which gave rise to local wits nicknaming the town 'Cas' Vegas and its sister town 'Ponte' Carlo.

Castleford is found at the confluence of two rivers; the Aire and the Calder. It is very likely that there has always been a settlement here as the river Aire begins a gentle meander at this point, making it the easiest place to cross. The Romans, very probably choosing to settle here for the same reasons, called it the 'place of bottles' in reference to the glass-making industry already based here. All kinds of glass bottles were made in Glasshoughton and then shipped around the world. The last glass factory in the town, United Glass, survived until 1983.

On the riverside is a flour mill, established in the 12th century, and although now long since mothballed, it remains the largest stone ground flour mill in the world. Clay mining started here in the 16th century, upon which a thriving pottery industry was built, established by the appropriately-named John Clay, whose kilns burned with the locally-mined coal.

But if history is to be believed, something far more significant happened in Castleford even earlier than any of this activity. In 555 AD, the eye of the soon-to-be-appointed Pope Gregory was caught by some attractive slaves in a Roman market. They were "so fair-faced and golden-haired," that he enquired of the trader where they came from. He was told they were 'Angles' from Deira (Castleford was then included in the kingdom of Deira in Post-Roman Britain).

Famously, when Gregory became Pope, his first act was to send Augustine to England to convert the Angles. By the end of the 6th century, Christianity had been reintroduced to England, and the then King, Ethelbert, was a convert. One could therefore maintain that the people of Castleford had a profound, if disproportionate, influence on the course of England's religious history.

What is not disputed, however, is the influence that coal mining had on both the history of Castleford, as well as the course of our story. Coal has been mined in Yorkshire's forty-plus coal seams since medieval times, with an early chronicler noting how lucky the locals were:

"Though here be plenti of wode, yet the people burne much yearte cole bycawse hit is plentifull and sold good chepe."

More logical spelling has evolved since then, thankfully!

During the industrial revolution, demand for coal was high and 'fuelled' the development of Castleford's manufacturing industry. In its industrial heyday, the town had a coking plant, brickworks, a chemical factory, and a power station, as well as potteries and glass-making kilns, all of which were reliant on a plentiful supply of coal.

There was a rush to open new mines. Of the one-hundred-and-fifty mines in Yorkshire at the end of the 19th century, twenty of them were situated within a few miles of Castleford. These mines were extremely labour-intensive, and workers were attracted from nearby counties. It was boomtown in Castleford, and the population soared from one thousand to fourteen thousand.

Joseph Noon was one of these itinerant coal miners who came to Castleford from Shipleywood in Derbyshire. He wasted no time in marrying a nineteen-year-old local girl called Harriet on Christmas Day, 1872. Harriet was the daughter of a farm labourer and could neither read nor write, signing her name with a cross in the marriage register.

The happy couple set up home in Watson's Yard, Castleford, close to Glasshoughton Colliery, where Joseph found work as a coal hewer. Just a few years later, however, Harriet died and, in circumstances that were to be repeated later in this story, Joseph's brother John came with his wife and children from Derbyshire to live with the recently-bereaved Joseph. Their arrival was, no doubt, very welcome as John and his wife, Mary Ann, helped to raise Joseph's children – seven-year-old Richard, five-year-old Mary, and four-year-old John –

alongside their cousins. It doubtless helped that Mary Ann was a baker's daughter and so almost certainly had the skills needed to feed her extended family.

John had worked down the pit since he was sixteen, as did his brothers and his father, Richard, and grandfather (another Joseph) before him. John first accepted a job at a newly-sunk Peckfield Colliery, but it wasn't long before he joined his brother at nearby Glasshoughton Colliery and settled into a house at 89 Temple Street, Half Acres, another suburb of Castleford. This was a 'two-up, two-down' terraced house.

These modest residences were built to cater for the rapid urbanisation of the industrial revolution. There were two bedrooms upstairs and two rooms downstairs. The early ones had toilets in the backyard that were shared between six families, who also took their fresh water from a shared tap. It's not surprising that these types of houses were soon to be targeted in the slum clearances of the 1930s.

Sadly, John died at the relatively young age of fifty-one. We don't know how he dies, but mining was a dangerous profession, and miners' lives were often cut short by accidents from rock falls, explosions, drowning as a result of flooding and lost limbs caught in machinery. If an accident didn't befall you, there were occupation-related illnesses such as black lung disease, a consequence of inhaling coal dust.

During his short life, however, John and his wife Mary Anne managed to produce ten children: William, Mary Anne, John, Daniel, Richard, Emma, Arthur, Joe, Harry and Tom. It was a time when large families were the norm. Thankfully John didn't survive long enough to know that the son who bore his name, lost his life in Flanders Fields, France in 1916 as a soldier in the First World War.

Our story now turns to John and Mary's fourth child, Daniel, born in 1886. Unsurprisingly, like his coal-hewing brothers and now generations of Noons before him, he started work at the pit when he was just thirteen.

Conditions in the mines before the First World War were very bad, and wages were pitifully low. There was no transport to the pit so early in the day, so Daniel would have to rise at 4 am to walk to his ten-hour shift, wearing only thick moleskin trousers for protection and clutching his 'snap' of bread and dripping, enclosed in a tin to protect it from rats.

His first job was to collect a safety lamp from the lamp cabin. The flame was captured inside the lamp to prevent it from igniting any gases that may be present down the mine. Leaving nothing to chance, the lamp keeper had a foolproof way of testing if the lamp flame was sealed; he simply blew around the flame to see if it flickered!

The miners were lowered down the pit shaft to the bottom in a cage attached to a winch and a huge winding wheel. This winding gear, fixed high above the pit shaft, is the defining feature of every coal mine and a reminder of the hardship miners endured. Glasshoughton Colliery was sunk in 1869, with the deepest shaft being 828ft. At a speed of 20ft per second, it would take less than one minute for the miners in the cage to reach the bottom of the pit, located beneath thousands of tons of solid rock. The darkness at the bottom is hard to describe. To the more imaginative mind, it would be hell on earth. The lamplight cast eerie shadows on the walls, and the eyes of the resident rats, often, reflected back the light.

Daniel's initial job in the mine as a pit lad, was to scrape and shovel up coal dust into tubs to reduce the risk of the dust igniting and causing an explosion. This work was undertaken at night after the miners had finished their shifts. He was tasked with a set number of tons to shovel before he could finish his shift in the morning. Daniel would have to get used to working in the dark, all alone and permanently terrified his light would extinguish, either because the oil had run out or the wick was too high, staining the glass black and rendering it opaque.

Older, experienced miners worked together in small groups, and at the age of fifteen, Daniel was eventually assigned to one of these teams. The pit floor resembled a huge spider's web, and arriving at the bottom of the shaft, the teams headed down separate roads sometimes walking miles to find their places of work.

In those days, the coal was hewn by hand using picks, hammers and wedges. It was hard work, and it was fiercely hot down there. The seams were sometimes only 2ft high, which meant that miners had to lie on their stomachs to hew the coal, erecting roof props along the way. It was difficult, dangerous, back-breaking work, and there's no doubt Daniel was sustained in this horrendous task by his faith in God.

The miners were paid by each ton of coal they produced, so teams worked closely together to ensure that they all pulled their weight. They looked after their team members, but injuries and illnesses were frequent. Soft hands could develop a 'beat hand' – a painful carbuncle on the palm. In fact, hands were frequently calloused and some remedied this by rubbing them with tobacco. However, there were few absences from work, because there was no sick pay. Miners simply couldn't afford to be ill.

Daniel's first role in his new team was as a pony driver. His task was to shovel the hewn coal into tubs that ran along tramlines at the side of each road. The ponies would haul the tubs to the surface with steel ropes. Remarkably, very young children and women did this coal-hauling job until, in 1842, the Victorians made it illegal for Women at least, to be employed in this way. When Daniel started working down the pit children had also been replaced by ponies.

Pit ponies often saved the miners' lives by alerting them to an impending roof fall they had heard or sensed, long before anyone else.

The pit ponies were as individual as the miners themselves, and Daniel had to learn how to work with his equine colleague (without the benefit of using reins), as their lives depended on each other. The heavy tubs of coal frequently overturned, and there was little chance of survival if either the lad or the pony were pinned against the coal seam walls.

Coming from the Welsh hills or the New Forest, these hard-working and strong ponies were clever too. They often saved the miners' lives by alerting them to an impending roof fall they had heard or sensed, long before anyone else.

Despite being permanently housed in stables located in the mine, the ponies were well cared for. Once a year, when the mine had a two-week holiday (or more frequently if there were strikes), the ponies would be brought to the surface where they would enjoy some well-earned leisure time in a huge field, where the locals would bring them potato scraps to eat. There were over three-hundred ponies at nearby Fryston Colliery, so it was often quite a spectacle to see them all together.

Daniel continued to advance in his mining career until he eventually reached the top job in his team – Coal Hewer – and life became settled.

At twenty-one, he married Hannah Elliot, who was a year his senior. She 'weren't from round ere' though. Hannah was born in Hartshorne (pronounced 'Hart's horn') in the neighbouring county of Derbyshire. It is unclear how they met, but sometimes Daniel had to look further afield for colliery work as employment in the mines ebbed and flowed in parallel with the demand for coal. Both being regular churchgoers, he would attend the local churches wherever he was working, and it was likely that Hannah moved in the same Christian circles.

Following in the family tradition, the young couple married at Castleford All Saints Parish Church in July 1907. There was no one to give Hannah away on her wedding day as her father, Jonathan, a labourer, was no longer alive. However, her sister Matilda was a witness to the event. Daniel's father, John, had also passed away by the time the wedding took place. Nevertheless, the happy couple settled a mile away from his widowed mother and siblings' home at 31 Healdfield Road in another two-up, two-down.

Incidentally, around this same time, another young man was growing up a short walk away. He was also the son of a miner, the seventh child of eight, and his name was Henry Moore, who became Britain's best-known sculptor. Like Daniel, he lived in the shadow of the Glasshoughton muck stacks and would attend the same primary school. However, their lives went in completely different directions when Henry won a scholarship to Castleford Grammar School and resolved to become a sculptor after learning about Michelangelo during a Sunday school lesson.

It can only be surmised that Henry harboured no fondness for his Castleford roots, as it took him until 1980 to make a gift of one of his sculptures to the town – and even then, he seems to have chosen the smallest one he could find! The feeling seems to be mutual as his hometown has had a memorial built to him on the site of his house that is so brutally ugly, it can only have been designed to ensure no one would ever want to visit it.

Daniel and Hannah had now moved to 3 Leaf Street, a few step from his family home and had started a family of their own. The firs to arrive was Harold, followed two years later by Freda and baby Herbert, who sadly didn't survive a year. Barbara was born shortly after, but tragically in 1915, when Barbara was only two-years-old Hannah died unexpectedly.

The First World War was raging, and Daniel could only be thankful that his profession had exempted him from being called to serve. However, he still found himself in an unenviable position having a difficult, dangerous job and three mouths to feed. Could he really ask his mother to look after his children as she had done for hi Uncle Joseph's?

Thankfully, an offer of help came from an unexpected source Hannah's younger half-sister, twenty-three-year-old Maud Agnes sent word that she would come to live with Daniel to help look after both him and her nieces and nephews.

Happily, within a year, Daniel - who was now thirty - had proposed to Maud Agnes, and he returned to Castleford Parish Church to marry once again. Maud Agnes's younger half-sister, Matilda, once again bore witness to the event and Maud's mother, who had since remarried, brought her new husband, George. He worked as gardener on the estate of Repton School in Derbyshire, where she was a char lady.

The newlyweds would go on to have eight more children, naming their first Hannah, after Daniel's late wife, and their next child John, presumably in honour of Daniel's deceased father.

Daniel Maud, and their family saw out the rest of the First World War. With the economy and demand for coal as it was, Daniel was only working three days a week at the colliery, as this was all there was on offer in the cash-strapped 1920s. At times Daniel may well have been tempted to sign up with the armed forces, given how tough the conditions in the mines were, and with the promise of a smart, clean uniform, pay of a shilling a day and the chance to return home a hero. Keeping chickens and pigs in the backyard helped to keep the family's head above water, but something had to change.

Dare to be a Daniel

Daniel harvesting corn with a scythe.

Chapter 2: Off the Rails

In 1922, at the age of thirty-six and fed up with the reduced hours at the pit and the uncertainty of being able to provide for his large family, Daniel - along with Maud and their six children (the oldest was Harold, aged fourteen) - set out on a courageous new adventure. Daniel had it in his mind to set up a smallholding: a farm or market garden to grow vegetables and to keep more animals.

At Glasshoughton Colliery, where Daniel worked, he heard that parcels of land owned by the colliery were available for rent. In those days, the collieries were privately owned, and after making enquiries, before long, he had agreed to rent a 7.5-acre site adjacent to the colliery. The rent for this land was very cheap and much less than renting his little council-owned house.

This specific piece of land was previously known as Carr Wood. The trees had since been cut down, and the timber had already been sold for profit. However, the tree stumps needed to be removed before the land could be used for anything else. This was the reason the land was so cheap. It was tough work but made easier once Daniel had borrowed a *Sylvester* from an ex-pit colleague. This ratcheted rope device, invented by a Derbyshire miner called Walter Sylvester, was used to safely pull out the pit props from tunnels before the ceiling collapsed with the potential to fatally injure the retreating miners.

Dare to be a Daniel

With stumps finally removed, Daniel's land was ready for tilling and planting, but he still needed a roof over his family's head. I wasn't long before he spotted the perfect solution. One day while reading the local newspaper in the library, as he did once a week, an advertisement posted by a railway company caught his eye. 'Retired railway carriages for sale - £10'. Daniel instantly saw the potential for converting one into a dwelling. He wasn't the only one who recognised this opportunity either, with two or three other local people snapping up the carriages. One located on Aketon Road, Cutsyke surviving well into the 1970s.

The Victorian steam-railway companies selling off their newly invented coach carriages as they became obsolete was a phenomenon of the 1920s. The Prime Minister at the time, Lloyd George, promised to return WW1 soldiers and their families to "homes fit for heroes," but this was not to be; with the housing shortage so great, the supply of new council homes was not sufficient to meet demand. A cheap-to build railway carriage bungalow subsequently filled the housing gap for some in the 1920s and '30s.

In Shoreham, West Sussex, ninety carriages, originally intended as net stores, were set down on the spit of land at the mouth of the River Adur. They were converted into bungalows earning the name Bungalow Town. The settlement even attracted some celebrity residents and, home to its own film studio, it was touted as the British Los Angeles. However, the studio's life was short-lived and was closed in 1922. In 1940, fears of a German invasion following

Dunkirk (or maybe it was just the opportunity the establishment wanted to clear unpopular, unregulated development so close to the sea) led to the government giving the owners just two days' notice to leave, with most of the bungalows subsequently demolished.

Daniel's 40ft x 8ft former steam-hauled coach carriage was delivered by the obliging railway company to the nearest railway sidings at Cutsyke. It became Daniel's responsibility from that point. He had managed to acquire two dray carts with low, detachable low sides. Quite how he managed to get the carriage onto the carts is anybody's guess, but no doubt he would have had friends, pit colleagues as well as family to help him.

The carriage continued its precarious journey by horse and cart down through the village of Cutsyke. It then turned left at the crossroads with The King Billy pub towards North Featherstone. Although there was a quicker route, this one was the best way to get it to the final location via a muck lane. This track led from North Featherstone to an extensive disused quarry overgrown with trees. However, despite its lush vegetation, the quarry continued to be used by the mining company to store their explosives, and the road leading to it had to be smooth and broad, as befits vehicles transporting gunpowder!

Why the carriage was placed where it was, nobody is entirely sure.

To safely reach the quarry, the horses had to pull the carriage across a field and through a previously-created gap in the hedge, before it came to rest some 15ft from the boundary. It was then shifted onto a raft of 5ft high barrels, four of them on each side.

Why the carriage was placed where it was, nobody is entirely sure. The distance of 150 yards from the nearby spring was probably important, or perhaps the horses had just simply had enough and dug in their hooves mulishly, refusing to move any further. Whatever the reason, this unusual five-compartment dwelling was the start of an exciting new adventure in the lives of Daniel, Maud and their still-burgeoning family. They had a roof over their heads (of sorts), freshwater, and precious land to farm and feed them. They also had faith that God would look after them if they continued to heed his word.

Daniel and Maud 1920s

Dare to be a Daniel

'Noonies' Carr Wood and their neighbours

Chapter 3: The Homestead

Carr Wood was roughly oblong in shape, huddled at the bottom of a shallow hollow beside a beck. The wood was bordered on one long side by a narrow beck, on the other, a hedgerow. Everything to the right of the beck gave way to an unrelenting industrial landscape. Out of view were the sewage works but darkly overshadowing Carr Wood itself was the Glasshoughton Colliery muck stack. This stack was made of shale, a composite of sand and stones left over from the coal mining process. Next to this, a short distance away was another mountainous waste pile of 'slag' from the coke ovens, another coal by-product used to fuel school boilers etc. This slag heap marked the far corner of Daniel's homestead.

Stand with your back to all this industry, however, and you'd be met with a bucolic scene of rich arable fields, country paths and hedgerows filled with wildlife and birdsong. These fields were owned either by the colliery or by the prosperous Featherstone farming family Copley, who still farm in the area today. But Daniel harboured a quiet ambition to one day farm these fields himself.

Beyond these fields, Pontefract racecourse came into view at the point where a sharp bend turns into the three uphill furlongs of the home straight. Racecourses are a symbol of Yorkshire, as it has the most of any county. Pontefract racecourse is as ancient as the land surrounding it, with Cromwell's soldiers reputedly watching races here.

Behind the hedgerow, at the bottom of a slope, was a freshwater spring. The water ran into an irregularly-shaped pond, previously gouged out of the landscape by the colliery, who had also placed a small pump house adjacent to the pond to take clean water all the way to North Featherstone Colliery. From here, the water was used to wash the coal and, some years later, the men as they emerged from their shift and headed for the pithead baths. Daniel was given permission from the land owner to put a stone slab beside the spring so that the sparkling, clean water could bubble up to the earth's surface, run over the slab and fall freshly into a waiting tin bucket.

From every other angle of the site, the colliery muck stack was in view. It was huge and, with its predominant colour being black, cast an ominous shadow over all its surroundings. Furthermore, it was alive with the continual thrum of overhead buckets moving down a mechanically suspended wire above the stack in order to dump their loads of waste. One of the tall standards that held the return wheel was situated immediately on the other side of the beck and was a permanent feature of the landscape. The waste bucket had two wheels that carried it along a wire until it hit an arm, which pivoted the bucket to discharge its load onto the stack. The load hit the stack with a satisfying 'pwoosh' sound, and the empty bucket then returned to the colliery - but not before issuing a few complaining creaks and whines as it resettled onto the wire for its return journey. As the heap got higher, the 'pwoosh' noise would lessen. These familiar sounds, sights and industrial smells were a constant accompaniment to life on this smallholding in the 1920s.

In the next five years, the Great War became a distant memory, and four more children had come along to make a total of ten. Child number nine was Denis, of whom more later. During that time, Daniel's unusual homestead had become well known. This was in no small part due to his many children who attended the local schools and Sunday School, as well as the result of the local business he had started, selling fresh vegetables and meat from his horse and cart. Carr Wood was by now referred to by locals as 'Noonies'.

Daniel, meanwhile, had been busy with home improvements. By now, he had replaced the barrels under the railway carriage with brick pillars. To do this without removing the carriage, he had dug down below the barrels to provide enough headroom in the living quarters. With his friends and children helping with the digging and shovelling the soil away, they created a brick-built living space beneath the carriage. The first-floor carriage now served solely as the family bedrooms, and Daniel and Maud now owned a two-storey fairy-tale home.

Surrounding the railway carriage, Daniel had also been busy building some brick outhouses for various husbandry needs. The most important building however was the smallest. Situated about 10 yards outside the front door to the right of the carriage, consisting of brick with a concrete floor, it featured a smooth wooden seat stretching right across the width of the building with a hole in the centre. This was the family toilet. As there were no loo rolls, newspaper cut up into squares was provided (although there was no regular newspaper delivery, so this was in itself a luxury!). Solids and liquids alike went down the hole.

In this period, all two up two down houses were arranged in rows back-to-back. If they were lucky, they owned their own toilet, situated in their backyard and called a 'dry midden'. An alley, just large enough to take a council lorry, ran between the rows of houses, and the middens were emptied during the night by workers who, in a testimony to British decorum, were called 'night soil men'. At the back of this little toilet building at Carr Wood was a trap door. The waste was shovelled out frequently (for obvious reasons, it didn't want to go much beyond a fortnight!) and spread onto the land. All the children took turns with this job as it formed part of their chores. It may be just a coincidence, but there was a lovely patch of rhubarb growing right next to the toilet!

Dare to be a Daniel

Jessie Noon marries Joe Owens, July 1943

(L-R Joe's mother, Peter,(child unknown)Ronnie Smith,Joe and Jessie,Hanna,Sophie -Harold's wife,Maud,Daniel and Freda's daughter Barbara)

Dare to be a Daniel

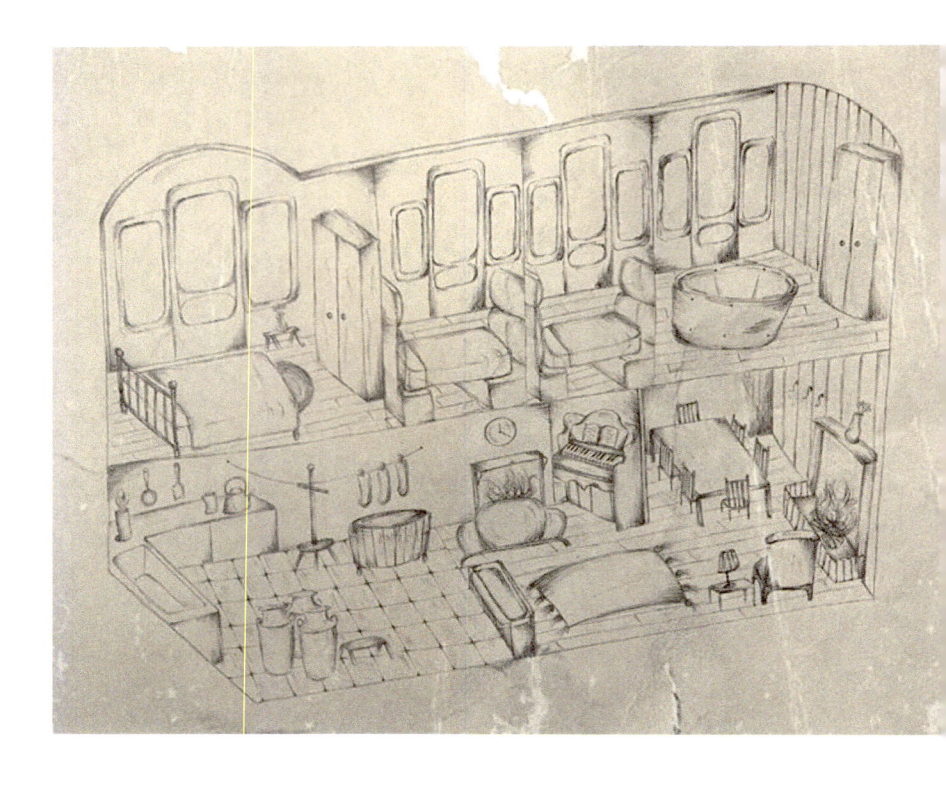

Inside the converted railway carriage

Chapter 4: A Converted Railway Carriage

Upstairs inside the railway carriage was the original 3ft wide passage along one side, with the original curtained windows and doors along the length. The corridor connected the former seating compartments. There were five compartments in total, the first two of which were knocked together to create Daniel and Maud's (or Dad and Mam's) master bedroom. All the other compartments had had their doors removed for ease of access, but with the kids regularly scampering up and down the new internal wooden stairs that began outside their room, the master bedroom had a curtain fitted across, for privacy.

For some time before Daniel had a chance to build the internal staircase, access to the bedrooms was via a hole in the floor of the carriage, where the children would be squeezed through every night to save them from going outside into the cold to ascend the outside stairs.

The next two compartments were bedrooms – one for the girls and one for the boys. The beds were made from slats of wood straddled between the original seats and stretching the entire length, as well as the whole width, of the compartment. A double mattress and blankets were perched on top of the slats to form a bed. Along with the presence of several sibling bodies, these beds ensured a snug night's sleep for all. The girls – Freda, Barbara, Hannah and Jessie – slept in the first room and then the boys – Harold, John, Danny and, later when they came along, Denis, Peter and Jimmy – in the next one.

The end compartment, with never-fulfilled dreams of being an internal bathroom, featured, among other things, a large free-standing bath however, it was only ever pressed into service as a bed for one or two kids to sleep in head-to-toe. The alternative and preferred bathing apparatus had handles, was made of tin and was propped up in the corner of the kitchen. That was until each until Friday night, when it was put in front of the fire in the living room and filled with water for everyone to use one after the other in descending age order, with Father first.

Portable paraffin lamps were used for light and heat. Candles were a fallback if fuel was scarce. Eventually, Daniel managed to buy and install a generator allowing electric lights to be used inside - something of a luxury for the time.

Downstairs underneath the railway carriage, Daniel had extended beyond the perimeter of the upstairs railway carriage to create a large living area. At one end was a brick wall with a Yorkshire range in the centre. This was coal black, about 5ft high, with a fire in the middle and an oven to the right-hand side. The fire was the only means of heating, and the kids would jostle with each other to get a chair next to it. The fire would be kept going all day to heat the water for washing and cooking.

The concrete floor was strewn with handmade rugs. This had one obvious advantage: there was no need to take your shoes off when you came through the door as the floor was easily swept clean. There was plenty of mud around though, as all the tracks around the homestead were muck. It wasn't until the 1920s that tarmac roads started to be built. Daniel never drove a car; he had a bike, and generally, the family would walk or cycle everywhere. The kids would wear wellingtons as they walked to school, but if they were going to church, they would hide their boots in the bushes at Cutsyke level crossings and change into shoes.

The living room was warm and comfy. There were armchairs and stools that would be pulled up to the fire and a small dining table which could accommodate most of the family at once. The brick walls had been plastered and covered in cheerful wallpaper. It was a lovely, cosy place to be and visitors commented that it was always spick and span. In the opposite corner of the living room was a sink where the water was kept for washing. The wash bowl was carefully shared as this sink had no tap; all the precious water had to be fetched from the spring in a bucket.

> *The vigorous pedalling of any generously-sized posterior always made for great amusement amongst the children, who described it as moving like "a bag of rabbits".*

Adjacent to the living area, Daniel had built a small sitting room with an open fire. This room just had space for a small sofa and Daniel's pump organ. Popular at the time, these organs featured two-foot pedals, which were connected to bellows. The keys operated reeds so that when the key was pressed, air from the bellows flowed up to the reed and made a sound. The tone and volume could be changed by using the stops – these were pull knobs situated behind the keyboard. The expression 'pull out all the stops' refers to using all the stops of an organ at the same time to create the loudest cacophony of sound.

These types of organs were used in all the churches at the time and were mostly positioned so that the organist's back was to the congregation. The organist had to keep pedalling and at quite a tempo in order to operate the instrument. The vigorous pedalling of any generously-sized posterior always made for great amusement among the children, who described it as moving like "a bag of rabbits."

However, in the railway carriage home, Denis has fond memories "of lying in bed, being lulled to sleep by Dad's mellifluous playing of the organ, accompanied by Mam singing hymns". Not long after, the sitting room would also be where the courtship of Denis and his sweetheart Lois was conducted. Denis, being the only child of Daniel and Maud to inherit the gift of playing the piano by ear, would try to impress Lois by performing popular tunes on the organ as best he could.

Behind the living area, but still underneath the railway carriage, the space was split into two rooms, both accessed from outside. On one side was the dairy, where Maud kept the milk from the cows and made butter. On the other was a washhouse. This had a 'dolly tub' which sat above a fire to warm the water for washing the laundry. Given the size of the family, you would think the dolly tub was in constant use. However, Maud instilled in her family a routine of changing clothes strictly after one week's wear to coincide with the weekly wash day (Denis still admits to finding it difficult to deviate from this regime more than ninety years later and lives in the hope that the neighbours haven't noticed how infrequently his smalls make an appearance on the washing line!).

The smell of roses around the door of the 'house' and bluebells in the wood are enduring memories of life in Carr Wood. Unless of course, the wind was blowing in the wrong direction, in which case there would be a whiff of the acrid smell of coke from the coke ovens!

Dare to be a Daniel

Peter, John and Denis 1930s.

Chapter 5: Noonies' Ten Thousand Kids

Daniel and Maud were decent, honest people, but the thing that fundamentally distinguished them from their peers was that they were active and committed Christians. Daniel had attended the non-denominational Salem Chapel near his home on Half Acres as a child, but there was a new religious movement sweeping the country whose influence among miners was profound.

The movement started in Dublin, where a group of disillusioned church ministers, rejecting the formality and hierarchy of the established church, formed a new denomination. They relied on Jesus's assurance that it didn't matter where they met; if they congregated in the name of the Lord, then the Holy Spirit would be among them and could inspire anyone to speak (at least brothers anyway, as

> *Bound together by their core belief that the Bible is the infallible authority of God, they discussed Bible truths in eloquent but simple language, addressing their prayers directly to God in their Yorkshire dialect, using phrases such as "God, thas no need to tell Thee anything. Tha' knows it all……"*

women, still weren't allowed to participate). In their plain meeting rooms, without the attendant statues and religious trimmings of church buildings, they were able to see that God was no longer just a remote, omnipotent figure in heaven. It appealed to the ordinary man that he was here in the room with them, and they could speak to him as they would to a real person. Importantly, no one man was above another, so they referred to each other simply as brothers or 'brethren'.

They rejected any one-man ministry, preferring instead to be guided by elders, while encouraging everyone to contribute because God has given everyone different gifts. With a rejection of organisational structure, the Brethren formed themselves into groups and referred to them simply as an 'Assembly' of people.

This group relocated to Plymouth and therefore became known to others as the Plymouth Brethren. This new way of worshipping was infectious, and it began to spread upwards and outwards throughout the country.

Daniel had accepted Christ as his saviour during a service at Salem Chapel, led by an evangelist visiting from a new brethren assembly in Pontefract. Following his conversion, Daniel and several other brethren were attracted to this new way of worshipping and attended the Breaking of Bread (or communion as it is more commonly known) at this assembly until there were 18 of them walking the three miles there and back every Sunday.

Many of the group were miners who, due to their harsh working conditions and the daily danger they faced, saw the need for powerful prayer and the comfort and hope this faith could provide them. Bound together by their core belief that the Bible is the infallible authority of

God, they discussed Bible truths in eloquent but simple language, addressing their prayers directly to God as a friend and in their Yorkshire dialect, using phrases such as "God, tha's no need to tell Thee anything. Tha' knows it all……We thank Thee that tha can see our troubles," etc.

In 1912 this group of enthusiastic believers, including Daniel decided to set up a new Assembly and following the Plymouth Brethren's lead, began to meet in each other's houses to break bread and discuss the scriptures. Their enthusiasm to share their love of God inspired them to hold Gospel meetings in various unusual premises including the Billiard Institute, the local primary school and rooms above 'The Bazaar' corner shop. They also preached fearlessly on the roughest of streets of Cutsyke, including Garth Street, notorious for drunken fighting after the pubs had closed.

Their work was richly rewarded as Assembly numbers grew and they believed that God was blessing their work. They continued meeting and evangelising in earnest in various secular premises, right through the first World War years when in 1920 when they were made an offer they couldn't refuse- the chance to buy an ex-army hut in Ripon.

At some considerable sacrifice, Daniel and these pioneers for God, managed to purchase the hut for £40 and a put down a deposit on a piece of land in Cutsyke on which to erect it. They had finally acquired a permanent home for their new Assembly and they called it simply

Cutsyke Gospel Hall. It was a small one-room building and it was just a ten-minute walk from the railway carriage.

Daniel contributed fully to the Assembly life by preaching the Gospel, but it was for a quieter role that he became best known. He put his personable nature to good use by visiting people who were interested to hear more about the good news of the Gospel. He really enjoyed engaging people in these spiritual discussions.

Maud also worshipped at the same Assembly and was a good singer in the choir. She would also preach, permitted to do so only to a congregation of women, at Scholes Hill Chapel in Methley. Maud was always kind and giving. Daniel, however, could be severe at times, but he was determined to instil Christian principles into his children and that involved imposing limitations and restrictions on worldly activities. His children were expected to be just, upright and decent and certainly not to tell lies.

As parents, Maud and Daniel were united in pursuing a spiritual existence and led by example in teaching their children to live a moral life. Daniel and Maud didn't smoke, and both were teetotal on principle. Similarly, their boys never went to the pub, even when they were older. Having had a strong work ethic instilled in them from an early age, all the children turned out to be good workers too.

As the Cutsyke Assembly didn't have a Sunday School, the numerous Noon offspring provided a welcome boost to the attendance at the Salem Church in North Featherstone, which did have one.

Dare to be a Daniel

To get to North Featherstone, the children trekked a mile or so across the fields (via land that would later become the M62), up the lane, past Copley's farm and The Bradley Arms. It was around a half-an-hour's walk –although that depended upon whether you had a fight on the way, in which case it took a bit longer. This is because there was a group of North Featherstone lads who took exception to 'Noonies' kids and, on one occasion, decided to accost them as they walked through the village on their way to Sunday School.

Spotting the Noon children coming, the assailants came running towards them shouting: "Noonies' ten thousand kids!" The Noonies naturally made their stand, stones were thrown, and the battle raged. Despite the ambush, the Noon children still got to the Sunday School on time – and the moniker 'Noonies' ten thousand kids' is still fondly remembered today.

A blind man played the organ at the Sunday School, and the ten thousand Noon kids learnt choruses that were committed to memory for the rest of their lives. One of the choruses they learned was *Dare to be a Daniel*.

It speaks about a young Jewish lad called Daniel, who stood up to King Nebuchadnezzar when he passed a law forbidding anyone to pray to anyone else except him. Daniel conspicuously continued to pray to God three times a day and was punished by being forced to spend the night in a den of lions. He was miraculously unharmed, preserved by the power of God.

Dare to be a Daniel

The song recounts Daniel's bravery and faith in seemingly impossible circumstances. Parallels can easily be drawn to our own Daniel, who ventured bravely into his new rural life, trusting in the Lord to take care of him. Equally, these words are prescient for his son Denis, as we will later discover. The chorus goes like this: -

Dare to be a Daniel
Dare to stand alone
Dare to have a purpose firm
Dare to make it known

Standing by a purpose true
Heeding God's command
Honour them, the faithful few
All hail to Daniel's band

Like most farmers, Daniel and his band of boys would rise early to feed the animals and milk the cows. The rest of the family would then get up and prepare breakfast. When they returned, Daniel would read the Bible to the family after they had eaten.

Daniel cultivated the land, growing potatoes, turnips and greens of all kinds, including sprouts and the *Cannonball* variety of cabbages. The children would be put to use cutting cabbages and stripping the sprouts from their stalk. Corn crops, particularly wheat and oats, were also grown in order to feed the horses and cattle.

Gradually, the young farming entrepreneur developed a greengrocery 'hawking' round in the villages of Westfields, Cutsyke,

Glasshoughton and Half Acres, where some of his relatives still lived. Daniel would go out with a dray horse and cart laden with his home-grown produce plus other goods bought from the wholesaler, including corn. This provided Daniel with ready cash and allowed him to finally be self-sufficient. The round first started on Saturdays only, before two further days were added during the week.

Denis recalls: "Dad would always go with one of his children, most often John. The family had regular customers, and if I was chosen that day to accompany Dad, I would knock on the door, take the order, bag it up and then weigh it on the scales. I used to enjoy doing it, meeting people and helping Dad make a profit. We kids were paid for our help in pocket money, usually about five shillings. Sometimes we would sell groceries to our grandmother on Temple Street, who could be relied upon to give us some bread and jam as a treat".

Daniel's hawking business was quite successful, and eventually, he had accumulated £1,000 in his bank account. He was so surprised at reaching this amount that he visited the bank and asked whether it was true. The teller confirmed it was and asked him if he wanted to withdraw the money. "No", was his response, "I don't want to take it out, I just want to LOOK at it!"

Daniel always kept pigs, which provided the family with a steady supply of pork, particularly through the war years. He also kept Campbell ducks on the pond, as well as geese who were effective at

Dare to be a Daniel

guarding as well as rounding up the children on occasion. He also kept goats for their milk.

Daniel built a brick cow shed to house about half a dozen cows. Along with the pigs and ducks, two horses eventually joined the menagerie. All the land was initially worked with these two horses - ploughing and carting – but as time progressed, a tractor replaced them as the prime workhorse on the smallholding. Daniel built three animal sheds for his pigs, cows and horses, situated 150 yards away from the carriage at the end of his land and adjacent to the public footpath. People often admired the animals as they walked past on their way to Pontefract Races.

> *The horses were much loved, and the children soon learnt how to hitch a horse to a cart or ride the animal – with no saddle – around the farm.*

The family got very attached to the farm animals too. The children kept pets, usually cats, who also had the job of keeping the mice at bay. Having no sheep, Daniel had no requirement for dogs, so they were discouraged as pets.

The horses were much loved, and the children soon learnt how to hitch a horse to a cart or ride the animal – with no saddle – around the farm. When bringing a horse back from the fields, they would always rather ride it than lead it. These were thick-legged cart horses, and one called Bob, was a grey. Once when Denis was in the field with his girlfriend Lois, he swankily hoisted her onto the horse – but rather embarrassingly, she promptly fell off.

But there was even more drama on the day one of the horses escaped its field and made its way to a field of oats, where it spent some time filling its belly. When he was discovered and brought back to the farm, Daniel made the grave mistake of giving him water, which made the oats swell. The hapless animal was soon lying on the floor in agony, his belly swollen to bursting point. Daniel sent Peter and John to run as fast as they could to fetch the local vet, but it was too late. With the horse in considerable distress, Daniel had little option but to dispatch it himself using the only means available to him– an axe to the head (gulp!).

Another of the children's daily chores was collecting a bag of coal from the muck stack before school. There were always pieces of coal to be found amongst the slag, and there would often be people on the stack coal picking. Occasionally word would get around that the slag was rich in coal, and people would arrive on their bikes to stand underneath the place where the bucket dispensed its load, ready to pick over the fresh waste. Daniel relied on this coal to keep the fire going, in order to supply boiling water for cooking and washing. There was never any gas or running water in the home. Ever resourceful, a thought occurred to Daniel one day that since Glasshoughton Colliery was only a stone's throw from Carr Wood, there might be an opportunity to mine his own coal.

He decided he would try to excavate some poor-quality coal, known as slag, which existed in seams not far from the earth's surface. This is called outcropping when it is done commercially. So, on an area of land behind the kids' play area, he began to dig a 15 feet-deep drift, or slope. At the bottom, he built horizontal tunnels leading away into the earth, and sure enough, he discovered plenty of coal there for the taking. The tunnels were all properly propped up as he had learnt how to do when he worked down the mine. He would chip out the coal with a sharp tool and bring the coal out in buckets. This coal was used to light the fire in the living room, the furnace to heat the pig swill and the water for the wash tub.

Daniel now had his own permanent supply of coal, and the Noonies kids had the best adventure playground ever! They loved to take their friends into the tunnels with candles or torches to show them "our mine." Denis recalls being given the fright of his life once when he was coming out of the drift with his friends, only to see an illuminated ghostly figure standing at the top of the slope. "It came as some relief to find that it was just our Jessie's friend Pansy Wilson under a bed sheet with a torch".

Daniel's family had all the food they needed as so much was grown or raised at home. Maud cooked everything on the range, but even with the girls enlisted to help, cooking for so many still took some doing. Dinner, eaten strictly at midday, consisted of potatoes, vegetables and meat. Occasionally a pig was killed on a special bench called a 'scratch', where it was also butchered, and there would be chops and loin for everyone. Likewise, the cows provided a source of beef, which would be stewed and served with suet dumplings, followed by steaming milk pudding made by Maud and the older girls.

Tea time would consist of a large plate of sandwiches, sometimes filled with either cheese, egg or dripping but more often with various preserves made after the harvest. Daniel would first say grace, and then a flurry of hands would make a grab for the sandwiches until the pile disappeared.

Maud was always busy with housework, whether it be washing, baking or ironing. Her principal job however was to ensure the groceries were all ready to be loaded onto the cart - and all this despite being pregnant every two years! Noonies kids knew they weren't allowed to sit around idle, but they enjoyed their various chores. These included working on the land, and in the summertime, when it was light, it was expected that they work for one hour after school before they could play.

In the winter, there were winter greens to harvest, as well as animals to look after. Repairs were made on the stable and pig sty, and the hedges were also cut at this time of year. On Saturdays, the children worked all morning, as well as the morning of each day during the school holidays. Perhaps their favourite job was at harvest time, bundling up the corn in sheaves and tying them with another stalk of corn.

The Noonies kids loved their childhood days and especially loved the countryside. They knew the names of trees and bushes from their elders and parents. They were taught to snare rabbits with a wire noose called a 'snickle' whose hard-earned contents would provide a delicious stew for Maud to prepare, all year round.

Their favourite time of year, however, was spring, which was spent climbing trees and looking for birds' nests. The children had collections of birds' eggs but stole them on the strict principle of not 'slugging' the nest entirely. Taking just one egg, they believed, didn't cause the bird to abandon its nest. They would get particularly excited if they found a partridge nest, which they considered was something special. "If a partridge flew up in front of you," explains Denis, "you would know the nest was near and would keep looking until you found it".

The children didn't lack for friends from Westfields and Cutsyke villages, boys and girls with long-obsolete names such as Walter, Ernest, Clifford and Winifred. Friends would love to be invited along to Noonies to roam the fields, climb trees, and jump ditches. In summer, they would swim in the freshwater pond and in winter, when the pond froze over, they were ideally equipped in their metal-soled boots and, with just a short run-up, to slide from one side to the other. Noonies friends returned home with scuffed knees and scratched arms and their mothers wondering, no doubt, what they had been up to.

"Mischief night – 31 October – was all part of the fun," Denis recalls. "We would play tricks on each other, and in the village, we had a trick whereby we'd fix a rattle with string to the outside of someone's window. Positioning ourselves a good way away, we'd then pull the string to bang the rattle against the window in an effort to get the inhabitants to come out of the house."

> *On Christmas Day one of our ducks would be served for dinner but there was no Christmas tree as Daniel wasn't convinced that the festive decorations were "scripturally based".*

Autumn's outstanding highlight, however, was bonfire night. "We had enough land to have a big bonfire," adds Denis. "Mam would cook potatoes in the bonfire and bake sticky Parkin, a sweet gingerbread cake Yorkshire is famed for. Weeks before the big night, our ongoing pastime was gathering timber for the fire from the hedgerows and trees. We would warn our friends not to raid our firewood as we were determined that *our* bonfire was going to be the biggest It usually was. Typically, it reached about 15ft high with a Guy Fawkes perched on top".

Noonies kids also loved Christmas and, like every other child, were full of anticipation and sleepless the night before. There were carols sung around the organ and Denis recalls being woken in bed one Christmas Eve to the sweet sound of *Silent Night* being sung by a bunch of carol singers, who had trekked across the dark fields to sing outside the railway carriage as the family slept. "As the melodic harmony faded into the night, the magic was broken by the sharp voice of one of the singers, 'Mr Noon, I've left some potato peelings on the side for you for your pigs', she bellowed!"

On Christmas Day, there were stockings on the beds, and the children were delighted if theirs contained an orange. One of their ducks would be served for dinner, but there was no Christmas tree as Daniel wasn't convinced that the festive decorations were "scripturally based". This is a view that Denis shares: "I think he was correct, and there were no presents from him on Christmas Day for the same reason," he says. "But on that day, Dad would come to all the kids and give each of us some money, so he couldn't quite divorce himself entirely from the Christmas custom!"

On Christmas morning, it was traditional for the kids to head to Barnes Road for carol singing. It was because a high-ranking official at the local chemical factory, Hickson and Welsh, lived in a large house there. On Christmas morning, he sat in the porch of his house with a pile of new pennies, dispensing a coin to everyone who sang a carol. A penny was roughly equivalent to 50p today, and Denis and his many siblings went every year and no doubt cleaned him out.

There was always a quota of Noonies at any given time attending the local school, but this seems to have been no apparent help to Denis on *his* first day at school, as he recalls:

"I was the first to arrive on the first day at infants' school and was told to go into the classroom, where there were desks with a seat attached to each one. My first thought was that you sat on the desk and put your feet on the seat – and that's how I was when the teacher came in! I still remember how they all laughed at me and how it spoilt the rest of my day

I was competitive, and I liked learning – and I loved Gym above everything else. I excelled in maths but preferred geography over history. I particularly loved Stoolball, an ancestor of cricket. It's where the two wickets are replaced by a wooden 5ft post with a square at the top. A bowler throws a small hard ball at the wicket, which is defended by a player holding a large ping pong type bat. As with cricket, the rest of the team fields to try to run out the batsmen. I was in the rugby league team and sometimes objected to going hawking because I wanted to play rugby. I played the 'stand-off' position, where my role was to get the ball as it came out of the scrum and pass it down the line

At home our Jessie was always happy to play with us boys because the other girls were much older, and there were fewer of them. She liked to engage in a game of daring, and when we went for a walk, the dare would most often be to jump the brook. There were always a number of bicycles in the house too, and on Sunday mornings, we would cycle quite a long way to Marston Moor near York where Oliver Cromwell first defeated the Royalist army in 1644. But more importantly to us, we knew that primroses always grew by the side of the road there and we would pick some and bring them back for Mam.

There weren't many books to be found lying around the converted carriage, but the family did have a Bible Concordance. This is a book that lists all the important words in the Bible alphabetically and is invaluable for planning sermons, even though it is by no means a thrilling bedtime read! In the evenings, we would play draughts, never chess, and Dad would challenge us as we competed for a space by the fire. When anyone went down to the town, they would bring a newspaper back for Dad. He wouldn't have a radio as he judged that it would unduly influence the family's views on worldly things. In this respect, we were more removed from the world to a greater extent than other families.

Apart from the Gospel Hall, school and the hawking round of vegetable sales, visits were limited to Castleford town centre. My first memory of Castleford was on a visit to the library, aged four. Upstairs was housed all the newspapers, and dad would use them to catch up on the events of the day without having to buy one. Since reading in silence was required upstairs, children weren't allowed. Dad told me to remain on a bench opposite the bottom of the staircase. I was clearly impressed by the majesty of these stairs ascending to the sky – I told my mother that night that 'I had been all over the world'.

We visited the seaside only once. It was to the nearest seaside at Bridlington. As well as Dad and Mam, the outing included all of us children. We had to walk to the railway station, and I remember to this day the anxiety that we wouldn't make it in time. From the train window, every hedge seemed to be full of lovely pink dog roses. Once there, we listened to the Cliff College choir singing on the stepped front as well as bathing in the sea and making sandcastles of course.

Once or twice a year however, we would go to Ackworth Hall. We always took a picnic – sometime pork sandwiches courtesy of one of our pigs. We would travel by bus to Purston and walk the rest of the distance. We played games in the spacious grounds of the disused hall, such as races and rounders. We were grateful to the rich families who had once owned the great estates that we could later benefit from.

Although we knew we were poor, we felt rich in that we loved our adventurous life in the countryside. We had a loving family and friends, and together we had a common purpose in running the farm. Thanks to my dad Daniel's courage, we had been freed from the terrible inevitability of working down the mine. We could now look forward to long and healthy lives ahead. What a gift we owe Dad."

Dare to be a Daniel

Daniel ploughing outside lion-tamer Bill's caravan.

Chapter 6: Neighbours and Careers

It wasn't long before Daniel was able to buy the 7.5-acre Carr Wood and rent more fields in addition. Denis continues the story in his own words:

"In total we had 40 acres of land, most of which we farmed. We continued to sub-let some of our land to two neighbours.

Mr Hoof and his wife lived on one side of the railway carriage. He had 2.5 acres and tilled his land by hand with fork, hoe and spade. His great skill was to grow daffodils and, when they were in bloom, Noonies kids would help sell them around the village of Glasshoughton in wicker baskets. The Hoofs' house was an ex-army hut measuring about 40ft by 15ft. They had a projecting canopy which provided them with storage space and they also had a well. Their family consisted of two boys and a girl. John was the younger boy and was at school with me. The eldest boy was a miner – Stan – and he was killed in a mining accident, unfortunately a very common occurrence in those days.

Then there was the wife of Mr Hoof. If the children weren't home, her method was to shout for them from the front door. She would yell 'STAN-LEY' in a loud, high-pitched voice which tailed away at the end.

Dare to be a Daniel

Our other next-door neighbours were the Ritsons and they had just half an acre. They were also Gospel Hall folks and Mr Ritson was a small humble man. Much to his sorrow though, his wife became a backslider, the name given to one who lapses into sinful habits. Her preferred habit was to spend a lot of time in the Working Men's Club in Cutsyke. In contrast, Mr Ritson was an early convert at the Cutsyke Assembly and figured greatly in the founding of the Yorkshire Sunday School Camp, of which more later.

Another neighbour, the Newboulds, had a wooden building beyond the land that Dad rented. They specialised in different kinds of poultry and had a well, so they didn't use our spring. But they sometimes had to fall back on coming to us for water. Their eldest son Arnold was my brother Peter's age and he took up as an apprentice butcher in Castleford market. Eventually the Newbould family bought the shop and Mrs. Newbould helped in it. They did very well in butchery.

> *One of the unusual characters who lived in these exotic gypsy caravans was known as 'lion-tamer Bill'. He used to work at the circus and was injured in the course of his taming (or so we liked to believe), leaving him with one eye and a bad limp.*

Further away from the house was what we called the 3.5-acre field. If Dad ever met anyone and they asked if they could stay on his land he never refused, and this is where he would put them. On one occasion he permitted a family of gypsies to take up residence. It was the beginning of the Second World War and they stopped travelling and stayed put there in two caravans facing each other. We were impressed with how elegant and clean these caravans were and how delicate was the lace they used for decoration. A lot of lace was also used to dress their horses that were tethered on the land in front of their caravans. We enjoyed playing with the gypsy children, who would buy vegetables and meat from us."

Denis continues:

"Another unusual character who lived in a gypsy caravan in this field during the war years. He was known as 'lion-tamer Bill', who used to work at the circus and was injured in the course of his lion taming (or so he had us believe), leaving him with one eye and a bad limp. He lived with his dog called Spider – a shaggy long-haired dog who accompanied him wherever he went. Bill came to buy groceries from us frequently and Mam served him. It was to her that he unveiled his colourful life story. Despite his diminished eyesight he kept a gun for hunting and wasn't averse to wielding it playfully when any of my sisters' amorous suitors approached across the fields.

It was in the corner of this field where Bill lived that Dad made a corn stack next to his caravan, so Bill was much in evidence when the threshing season started. He had a kindly disposition and could be relied upon to help out with the harvesting and stacking the corn for winter. Combine harvesters – which combine the reaping, threshing, gathering and winnowing processes into one – weren't available then but one day every year Dad would hire a threshing machine from

Smiths of Altofs. This machine would beat the corn to separate the seed from the husk and stalk, known as 'chaff'.

As a young boy I had to collect the chaff, which was a horrible job as the tiny pieces got everywhere, even under your clothes. However, my elder brothers John and Peter saw an opportunity for a lucrative side line; they made an offer to take over Smiths' business and started a business threshing for other farmers at harvest time. They took along some of my brothers to help out. Peter was set on the idea of becoming a farmer, but our market garden business wasn't big enough to accommodate another pair of hands, so he became an apprentice on a farm owned by a Mr Richards in North Featherstone. John initially worked down the mine but eventually came into the family business, and along with Peter, they carried on farming together for years. Peter bought Mr Hoof's hut when he died and raised his family there.

My brother Danny, despite being his father's namesake, didn't get on well with the rest of the family and a lot of unpleasant arguments developed between him and Dad. He was the black sheep, rebelling about his place in the family hierarchy and complaining about having to do mundane chores. He would frequently grumble about something he didn't want to do and was constantly fighting with John. It was these three brothers, however – John, Peter and Danny – who, between them, worked the farm with Dad. The remainder of the older children, meanwhile, began to leave home to look for work.

In June 1927, Harold, as a young man of nineteen and just six weeks after I was born, embarked on the Cunard steamship *Ausonia*

Dare to be a Daniel

from Liverpool to Canada. He found work as a labourer on a large farm estate in Montreal, where he learnt to fell trees and handle timber. During the winter months, when work on the estate dried up, he trained as a Log Roller. This was the highly dangerous skill of guiding floating logs downriver by balancing on top of them. He returned home aboard the same ship three years later in November 1930 and got a job on a farm in Morley, Derbyshire, where he employed his newly acquired lumberjack skills.

Communication while working away from Carr Wood was not as efficient as it might have been and, on one visit home to the family, Harold dropped the bombshell that he had a wife. He had married a girl called Sophie, a German Jew who fled from Europe after her parents were killed in a concentration camp. They were both employed on the same estate, eventually setting up their own successful tree felling and timber business in Syston, Leicestershire. Appropriately, Harold won a contract making pit-props for mines. Once he invited Dad and Mum for a rare visit away from the farm where they found Harold and Sophie happily living in two caravans and the proud owners of an old V8 car. Sophie did all the cooking outdoors until eventually Harold bought a smart bungalow, where they lived out a happy and productive life.

For his eldest daughter Freda, Dad thought the safest career was to go into service in a Jewish household in Kidderminster, Worcestershire, where he felt she would be free from worldly temptation in the employ of upright, respectable people. She was later employed as a maid to Lady Howard of Castle Howard, a fine historic country house near York owned by the Howard family.

Following her marriage to her husband Ernest, they were both appointed as head housekeepers and had living quarters in the house. At Christmas they would invite the Noon family to visit and spend the day in the great house with them. Freda's living room featured a grand piano, which came in handy at Christmas. On these occasions we were free to roam the ancient house with its ancient sculptures, and paintings by Joshua Reynolds and Thomas Gainsborough. There was always a huge, lavishly decorated Christmas tree in the house and roaring open fires that needed to be kept alight. To the Noon kids' delight, the Howard family also had a full-size dolls house to play in. The disciplined and upright Noon upbringing served the Howards well. Incidentally, the housekeepers' living quarters now serve as the tea rooms.

Barbara went into service in London to the house of a wealthy man who owned a yacht, on which she was occasionally asked to serve and, when she did, to wear a sailor's uniform. She was a kindly disposed, attractive person who sadly contracted TB, which was very common in those days. Barbara knew she was dying and wanted to spend her last days at the railway carriage. However, she was too ill to travel home by train, Happily, Dad was friendly with the local funeral director who offered to fetch her home in his hearse!

The next sister was Hannah, a slight girl with great aspirations for a better life. She liked to read comics but because they were no

Dare to be a Daniel

allowed, she would sneak one into the toilet and read it by the light of a paraffin lamp. Hannah also spent some time in service before returning home for a time, taking a job in a chemist shop in Pontefract. She cycled to work down Carr Lane, which involved quite a stretch of dirt track and which she found hard going. On a frosty day, she was wont to say that there is nothing more horrible than the frozen top surface of the soil which by evening had turned to soft mud. It was no better for her in the summer mind you, when the ground was hard, rutted and bumpy. The tide turned for Hannah when she served a man in her shop called Ronnie; friendship soon blossomed to love and they married –though not in the shop, obviously! Together they ran a hardware shop before taking over as the head housekeepers at Castle Howard, when Freda and Ernest retired, where Hannah at least had a glimpse of the life she had always aspired to lead.

Jessie was the youngest girl and she was a real giggler, always cheerful and fun. She didn't want to move away from home when it was her turn to find work, so she got a position at the local sewing factory. Dad had misgivings about this as he thought she would have to work among 'rough, foul-mouthed girls'. But she went anyway and managed to remain relatively refined despite mingling with the riff-raff.

At the peak there were ten of us living with Mam and Dad in the railway carriage and if that wasn't cosy enough, Mam's father, George Elliot, came to live with us in his later years, before he passed away in 1931. Like many Victorians before him, he couldn't read or write and so Mam would read to him every day. He had a favourite saying as he descended down the wooden stairs each morning, rubbing his hands and declaring in a shaky voice: 'Heavy dew this morning!'.

More than anything, I remember the converted railway carriage as a warm place, with the comforting presence of my Mam and Dad and the companionship of my large family."

Dare to be a Daniel

Harold (far right) working as a lumberjack

Denis and Lois in Scarborough during their courtship

Dare to be a Daniel

Chapter 7: Denis Noon's Story

"War broke out when I was twelve and I clearly remember the day that Paris fell in 1940. I was thirteen and coming home from school, just a twenty-minute walk door-to-door. I had reached the Cutsyke level crossing when some pals shouted across to me that the city had capitulated. I couldn't believe that the mighty capital of France was overcome. It was of course the end of the occupation of Europe by the Allied Forces, a road that led to Dunkirk and the evacuation of our troops from the French mainland.

The Second World War affected us all. The family discussed world events around the kitchen table and was to dominate six years of childhood discussion: When our bombers were setting off to Germany from the RAF base at Sherburn-in-Elmet Airfield, they would circle above Carr Wood, lining up ready to set off. We could hear the drone of the engines and it brought home to us starkly how close the fighting was.

The war had seemed distant until a single bomb was dropped on Castleford, landing on our friend Jean Aldersea's house, but thankfully no one was hurt.

The 8th Army in North Africa occupied our thoughts for much of the time and we heard a lot about Field Marshal Rommel, the German 'Desert Fox', who was extolled as an excellent leader of troops. But, of course, he represented the enemy who were attacking the Suez

Dare to be a Daniel

Canal in an effort to cut off supplies to the Allied troops. It was fortunate that Commander-in-Chief Field Marshal Montgomery was brought in to take over command of the 8th Army. This military force was fascinating as it was drawn from all corners of the British Empire, including India, Rhodesia and New Zealand. A route was devised to supply the troops from East Africa via Nigeria, where they steadily built up the armour for the big push back to Algeria from where Rommel retreated to Italy. It was all very exciting from our point of view.

We had rationing at home, but I don't ever remember going hungry – after all we had our own vegetables. You were allowed to rear and kill a pig – one a year or so – and so we had plenty of pork and Mother would bake our own bread too. Clothes rationing was in place and there was a lot of talk among the girls about how clothes could be obtained, one way or another. Fish and chip shops remained open and this was an occasional treat. Cinemas were the main entertainment of the day and Castleford was lucky enough to have four of them.

After happy years at Cutsyke Infants and Juniors but having failed the 11-plus to go to the grammar school, Ashton Road Senior School called. Then owing to my prowess at Maths, I'd managed to pass an exam to win a year's scholarship at the local technical school. Unfortunately, owing to the mysterious world of signs, co-signs and tangents, I tumbled from the top of the class towards the bottom. I did though manage to pick up a few engineering skills which secured me a job as a lathe turner immediately after leaving college in the winter of 1942.

That job entailed a round trip cycle to Wakefield each day of some ten miles. I also attended evening classes at Whitwood College several evenings a week. It was a bit of a hectic schedule and, even though I would hold onto the pole at the back of a double decker bus to give me a 'lift' up the hill from Normanton to Whitwood at the end of my cycle journey, the whole schedule had a detrimental effect on my health and I came out in nasty boils on the back of my neck. My father reprimanded me, and I resigned from the job, instead working with Dad on the farm until Spring waiting for my skin to be fully healed before looking for another position. This next role would turn out to be a major turning point for the rest of my life.

Harbouring dreams of becoming a carpenter, I enquired at local joinery firm Harry Robshaw to see if any jobs were available. Though there were no vacancies in joinery, I was instead offered one on the painting and decorating side. I was very happy because I was put with a foreman called Walter who was an engaging man who could tell a few interesting tales. I hadn't ever been acquainted with anyone so vocal and knowledgeable and I was intrigued. It was partly his personality that made me content, but I also enjoyed the work. It was a five and-a-half day week at the time at a wage of three pounds a week, which was considered a good wage for a craftsman in the 1940s. During the Second World War, it would go up to five pounds a week and we would all give some of our wages to Mam for our keep.

By this time more of the Noon brood had started to spread their wings. John was now married, having met his wife by learning to dance and practicing at one of the three dance halls in Castleford. Two brothers Arnold and Derek Roberts, who also worked at Robshaw's were good dancers and could always pick up the girls. I went along to the Co-Op dance on one occasion but felt a bit of a wallflower as couldn't dance. Then I remembered that a teacher at Whitwood College taught dance classes at lunchtime, so I went along. The teacher reminded us that, unless we learnt how to dance, we would miss out socially. She taught us the Palais Glide, a great dance where you stand beside your partner with arms crossed behind your back gliding left to right in time to the music.

I was very happy that day but was brought down to earth with a bump on my way home from college, when I experienced jealousy for the first time. A scholar at the college had a dad who was a builder and he drove past me in a car. I too really wanted to own and drive a car, but it would be another thirty years before I managed to fulfil that dream."

It was at work that Denis fell in love. He tells the story:

"Lois Jean Theasby (pronounced Lois rather than more common pronunciation, 'Lowis') was born in Airedale in 1929 but had moved with her parents to Featherstone. Her father Alf was a bus driver and had moved to the area from the seaside town of Scarborough to drive some of the first ever 'Motor Buses' that succeeded the trams (and which initially ran on solid wheels before the pneumatic tyre was introduced).Eventually Alf moved his family near to his local bus depot in Castleford. In 1937, when Lois was eight-years-old, her mother Frances had an affair with Alf's friend Frank and went to live with him, leaving Lois alone with her father. Alf advertised for a live-in housekeeper which brought a response from widower Mona Cowley, who came to live at 63 Ashton Road along with her beloved young son Donald. Not long after that, Mona and Alf were married but the following years were hard for Lois who, in the shadow of Donald, felt neglected and lonely.

> *Lois caught my eye as she had black hair and a beautiful smile, enhanced with scarlet lipstick.*

Like me Lois went to Ashton Road Senior School. We didn't know each other though, being two years apart. Lois went to the Methodist Church on Smawthorn Lane and became a Sunday School teacher. She'd left school at fourteen and was working in a dress shop on Carlton Street, Castleford and it was while I was painting the office at the back of her shop that I met her. Walter and I had painted the top and bottom half of the walls two different colours, as was the fashion, and my job was to create a dado effect by adding a line of paint between the two colours. Lois caught my eye as she had black hair and a beautiful smile, enhanced with scarlet lipstick. She was always busy dusting hats, arranging the clothing rails and serving customers. In Lois's presence, I admit, I found it hard to concentrate on getting the line straight!

I travelled to work on my bike and waited for Lois to finish work so I could walk home with her. I had to be sneaky, however, as Lois always left with her colleague Dorothy. The two girls walked together, only parting company at the end of Smawthorn Lane, whereupon I would cycle past Lois and pretend that it was just a coincidence bumping into her. On the first few occasions I just waved and shouted hello. This continued for a time and Lois soon realised what I was up to and decided that if I didn't stop to talk to her the next day, she would change her route home to avoid me (little did she know that since I was shadowing her from the outset, it didn't actually matter which way she walked home, I would have cycled past her regardless!). Thankfully, however, I got the message and did stop and chat; this was the start of our relationship.

There was a short period when I wasn't sure if I was her boyfriend or not as I heard that she had gone dancing with someone else. But finally, on a date to the cinema, it was eventually mutually understood that we were a couple. Lois recalled later that she was taken aback when she was first taken home to the railway carriage but noted that, since I had no shame in it, neither did she. In fact, she loved the warmth of the family atmosphere compared to her own strained homelife."

> **ADVERTISEMENT**
>
> CAN WE HELP YOU WITH YOUR ACCOMMODATION and MAINTENANCE PROBLEMS? .... CONSULT
>
> **HARRY ROBSHAW & SON**
> BUILDING CONTRACTORS
> GLEBE ST., CASTLEFORD
> —— Phone 2153 ——
>
> Specialists in
> **PAINTING &
> DECORATING**

Advertisement for Robshaw who first employed Denis as a painter and decorator.

The young paratrooper.

Chapter 8: 1945 – Denis' War Begins

A week after the war had finished – on April 17, 1945 – Denis received his call-up. He recalls:

"I received a letter calling me up for National Service. I was eighteen and enclosed in the envelope was a one-way railway ticket from Castleford station. I was the only one in the family to be conscripted, as the rest of my brothers were exempt because of their status as farmers. A few weeks later and with a crowd of familiar faces from Castleford, I boarded a train with my kit bag to Berwick-upon-Tweed, located on the border of Scotland and England. On the platform at Berwick station, we were met by soldiers who formed all of us new recruits into columns of three and walked us to the army camp.

I was proud to be in the army. I got up early to perform my ablutions with enthusiasm in an open-sided building containing rows of sinks. It was not much different from home, really. We slept in two-tiered bunks and I had the bottom berth. While I wasn't used to the new regime, I soon conformed to the different habits of others and managed alright, showing enthusiasm and doing as I was told. We soon became familiar with the bellowed commands of the corporal. He did drills of thirty men – a platoon – in columns of three and

Dare to be a Daniel

instilled into our brains all the commands associated with marching. If you did well, you were rewarded by being moved to the front rank.

My friend from Wakefield was in the top bunk and he would go to the NAAFI on Friday nights and get boozed up. Once, he came back and spewed up all over my bunk. It didn't spoil our friendship, but we went our separate ways at the end of the training.

While I wasn't a committed Christian at that time, I was in the habit of attending church. I found a warm welcome in Methodist chapels if I couldn't seek out a Gospel Hall.

The first six weeks of square bashing was the best time in my entire army service. Every minute of the day was taken up with one thing or another, be it lectures or shooting practice on the range. At the end of the training period, all of us new recruits looked and marched like proper soldiers.

At this point everyone was dispatched to other departments or regiments and there were lots of posters around the barracks encouraging people to join them. This was the first time I became aware of the Parachute Regiment; jumping out of an airplane appealed to me for some reason –and it also paid a bit more than other regiments! I was always trying to save up and by the time I came out of training, I had put aside some money. Most of the others had spent all theirs on drink and cigarettes.

To be honest, I didn't think about danger. I expected to fight and assumed that, when I had jumped from a plane, I would have no choice. So, when I was asked to go before the commanding officer for it to be confirmed that I was to be enlisted in the Parachute Regiment, I had no hesitation in accepting.

I had written regularly to Lois during my training and on a short leave before joining up with the Parachute Regiment for the first time, Lois and I went to John Lewis's in Leeds, where a series of black and white photos was taken of the dashing young soldier of the Airborne Infantry, 4th Battalion Parachute Regiment wearing the coveted maroon beret of the regiment.

It was only a short while after that that we had to report to an army depot in Shorncliffe, near Folkstone on the South Coast of England. There began ten weeks of intense physical training as the fitness level required for joining 4 Para is far higher than the level mandated for other Army Reserve Infantry units. It included assault courses and other military exercises as well as navigating, with and without a map! As part of our gym sessions, we all had to learn how to box, the first time I had done this. There was a notorious bully in our regiment, who coincidentally came from Castleford and, occasionally, the gym master would put pairs together to box in front of everyone – and one day he put me against the bully! To my surprise – and probably everyone else's – I beat him! This won me the admiration of the other recruits and earned me a place on the boxing team, where I was awarded a medal for my achievements.

Our parachute training started in earnest too. We were firstly taken to a former airport, where we were lowered from the top of a tower at a speed you would land when parachuting. This taught us how to land safely. We also learnt how to assess the landing spot; for example, if we were drifting, we would turn sideways to the drift by twisting the webbing above our heads. If the parachute got tangled we would kick our feet to unravel it.

For the next stage of our training, we were taken to an airfield where we practiced jumping out of a hot air balloon. The soldiers would get in, six to a basket, and the balloon would be floated up about 700 ft into the air. Our parachute line would be attached to a strong point in the basket and a door opened into the fresh air, which was where you jumped from. You were always made aware of how dangerous it was to jump with a parachute and all of us were motivated to learn how to do it properly, because it would mean the difference between life or death.

After completing our practice jumps, we would have a cup of tea from the tea hut. Without a doubt, I recall these being the best cups of tea of my life, and that was simply out of relief; we were alive! It was while we drank our tea that we watched our fellow parachutists leaping from the basket. The instructor would shout something loud – 'TIMBER!' was one of the words used – to give you both the courage to jump and to control your breathing. Jumping from a hot air balloon actually turned out to be much worse than leaping out of an aircraft. That was because, when you jump from an aircraft, you ride the slipstream backwards before you start to descend. From a hot air balloon, however, you drop straight down like a sack of potatoes!

Dare to be a Daniel

Once in the aircraft, I was invariably chosen to be the first jumper – someone who would be confident and give encouragement to the others. I must have been seen as someone who had courage but that was not always the case. I actually adopted 'Timber!' as my own jumping word to help me overcome my fear.

For the next stage of our aircraft training, we took to the air in a Dakota, a plane with a long fuselage. On its ceiling was a strong point with a rail and we had to form a queue and attached ourselves to the rail. The Dakota's door was on the side of its fuselage and those at the back shuffled forward as each person jumped. The jumper immediately behind you checked you had attached your line correctly and the instructor would be at the side of the doorway, patting you on the back to encourage you. One of our regiment was too scared to jump and, unsurprisingly, didn't make it to the end of the training.

The line was made of webbing and unfolded 20ft to 30ft before the force of your fall would undo three knots. These ensured that the huge circle of silk and hundreds of feet of fine chords wasn't tangled when it opened. When the final knot was untied, the webbing came away from the chute and then you were on your own, free falling from the sky. It was scary but thrilling.

Learning to land successfully was key, as you couldn't form a good fighting machine with the rest of your platoon if you sustained a broken leg or worse than that, land badly on your haversack which accompanied your precipitous fall, and into which was packed bullets, rifle and hand grenades!

Dare to be a Daniel

The WAAFS packed the parachutes. These women worked on long 30ft-40 ft tables that were spotlessly clean, so as not to damage the delicate parachute fabric. We went to see them in order to give us confidence in how carefully they packed our 'chutes. They were fully alive to their responsibility for another person's safety, knowing that the accurate packing of each chute meant the difference between life or death for us.

> *One day, a corporal burst into the barrack room and bellowed 'It's over, the war in Japan is over and something as big as my fist ended it!'*

Some airmen who survived a jump from a burning spitfire went back to thank the women who had packed their 'chutes, owing their lives to their skill.

Even though the war in Europe was over, the enemy was still the Japanese as far as we were concerned. We would practice charging and thrusting our bayonets into a sandbag and told the bag represented a Japanese soldier now, not a German.

One day, as I was about to finish with this part of the training a corporal burst into the barrack room and bellowed: 'It's over, the war in Japan is over and something as big as my fist ended it'. He was referring of course to the atomic bombs that were dropped on Nagasaki and Hiroshima. The Japanese capitulated knowing they were outmatched against 'The Bomb' and, in doing so, ended the Second World War.

We were jubilant but carried on as normal as the army still had a job to do. And as it turned out, because Britain was given the mandatory power over Israel, there was going to be a specific job for me to do too.

Parachutists had earned a reputation for courage and fortitude during the war and I was proud to be part of the regiment. I thought my parachute training was great: well organised, disciplined and tough. At the end of my training, I was presented with the regimental winged badge, to be worn on my right shoulder. They said to me: 'Now you have your badge you'll will be walking on the left-hand side of the road from now on'.

I was then drafted for a short spell to Aldershot barracks before – in 1947 – being dispatched to Palestine in the Middle East. Until I joined the army, I had only ever travelled as far as Yorkshire and its neighbouring counties, however I recalled the motto of the parachute regiment 'Utrinque Paratus' meaning 'Ready for anything' …and I was."

Dare to be a Daniel

Boarding a plane for a parachute jump.

Dare to be a Daniel

Denis wears uniform of the Airborne Infantry 4th Battalion Parachute Regiment.

Dare to be a Daniel

Denis with fellow army friends in Palestine.

Chapter 9: Service in the Middle East

Denis continues:

"We were taken by train to Dover, from where we crossed the English Channel and then continued by train to Toulon. Once in France, we stopped at some army huts beside the railway, where we were given food. I remember that we had white bread and that this was unusual, as we only had brown at home. At Toulon we boarded a boat to Port Said in Egypt, north west of the Suez Canal that the British had so recently defended from Rommel. Finally, we arrived at our destination, an army camp on the outskirts of the capital Cairo."

> *It was noticeably warmer, and we were issued with Khaki summer dress which included shorts – 'get your knees brown' the older squaddies would shout at us.*

It was noticeably warmer, and we were issued with Khaki summer dress, which included shorts. 'Get your knees brown,' the older squaddies shouted at us.

We were able to go about in Cairo in the limited time we had before being taken to the other side of the Suez Canal, where army trucks were waiting to take us to Palestine. We arrived in the very northern part of the territory – just north of Haifa, the port juts out into the Mediterranean and is where Palestine borders Syria. Here, we were shown to the tents which were to be our main accommodation for the next year.

I was called into the officers' tent one day to receive my promotion to Lance Corporal, which entitled me to one chevron on the arm of my uniform. Army staff were either non-commissioned or commissioned. As a non commissioned soldier, you started as a private without any authority, progressed to lance corporal with one chevron, two for a corporal and a sergeant had three chevrons. Add a crown and you were a sergeant major. Commissioned officers trained at Sandhurst and took exams alongside their physical training. These were posh folks, smart guys. They had a different system of insignia but you could usually tell them apart by the way they spoke.

While my promotion didn't protect me from square-bashing, it did mean that I would now be called upon to stand at the front to conduct the drills. I enjoyed this as I was able to raise my voice and lead the troops and maybe it was this experience that whetted my appetite for open-air preaching in subsequent years. But I was still a long way down the army hierarchy, and that was brought home to me cruelly one day. The privates had formed a rugby union team to play other units made up from the rank's ordinary soldiers. The officers were frequently old rugby types, who wouldn't normally mingle with the lower ranks, but the sport was irresistible to them and they pulled rank to join in. As a result, I got dropped from the games.

Entertainment as well as catering was organised by the NAAFI and was based in a large tent in the camp. This is where I sampled alcohol for the first time. The lads invited me to join them in the NAAFI – we often went there for 'tea and wads', slang for a cup of tea and a slice of cake – but I joined them on this occasion for a drink. Although I had hardly had anything to drink, I pretended to be drunk on the way home to make them laugh, weaving about and singing *Drunk Last Night and Sixpence,* the popular marching song of the day. And that, it turns out, was my last ever drink of alcohol.

At the end of the Second World War, the Allies repatriated over seven million Jews displaced by the Nazis. Most of these displaced people were in Germany and many didn't want to return to their own country, as anti-Semitism was still rife there. Many were housed in huge refugee camps where a strong movement was established among them, agitating for the creation of a Jewish homeland in Palestine. It was understandable they wanted their homeland; six million had lost their lives, and those remaining in Europe were trying to get to Palestine which they considered to be the historical homeland of the Jews and the only place they could escape anti-Semitism. A quota of refugees was given permission to enter Palestine, but numbers were limited, largely due to objections from the Arabs. Nevertheless, hundreds of Jews began flocking illegally to Palestine by boat and it was the job of the British forces to intercept these vessels. One big boat, the *Exodus 1947,* was loaded with four-and-a-half thousand Jewish passengers and the ship got as far as the beach at Haifa, where the occupants melted away into the town among the locals. The British forces cordoned off a large semi-circle around the town and sifted through everyone in that area to prove their identity. The ones that couldn't, were deported to a detention camp in Cyprus.

Our regiment was detailed to board the British ship that transported these people into exile again in Cyprus, where they would stay until the international community had reached a settlement regarding their futures. It was a huge cargo vessel with an open deck to the sky. We soldiers were on the top deck and our job was to ensure there was no trouble during the journey. I remember looking down into the hold and seeing hundreds of people huddled together below and having sympathy for their terrible plight. The ship anchored offshore in Northern Cyprus near the tourist resort of Famagusta, at which point everyone disembarked for their onward journey. We never left the boat.

Soon after, we moved to a new camp south of Haifa, but there wasn't much to do. I still enjoyed the discipline of the army, but my attitude had changed. I wanted to get home as soon as I could to experience something different other than sleeping in a tent and doing nothing. The army's purpose is to fight and if there is nothing to fight for, life is tedious. Little did I know that something was about to save me and give me a purpose.

I had made it known in the camp that I was a painter and decorator, and the army had already asked me to do a few jobs. I was put into the Pioneer Unit, which provided the manpower to work with army

Dare to be a Daniel

engineers on tasks such as the construction of road bridges, defences and water supplies. I had painted a few little directional signs around the place using the sign-writing skills I had learnt, which earned me a compliment from the commanding officer. Things started to look up.

The Pioneer Unit was housed in a separate hut beyond the perimeter fence, adjacent to an orange orchard. On one occasion, a fellow soldier and I took a walk and noticed a group of people picking oranges there. I started chatting with them as best I could, even though I didn't speak any Arabic. I just wanted to be friendly, and it was lovely to, at last, be with people who were living a normal life. One chap spoke English, and it proved that they were equally as European as us.

> *...a throng of people came down a street at right angles to the one we were in and kept on coming. We were commanded to 'fix bayonets', advance and charge at the crowd.*

He invited us to his home for a cup of tea, and the two of us went along. We had to keep our rifles with us, which was a bit of an embarrassment, but he introduced us to his wife and family and showed us great kindness and hospitality which I have never forgotten.

Not long after this, we were instructed to go to Tel Aviv as part of a peacekeeping force. Britain was the dominant power in Palestine, and immigrants continued to enter the State illegally. Two paramilitary Zionist groups, The Stern Gang and the Haganah, were fighting for the freedom of the Jews in Palestine. They believed that God had promised Israel to them and considered this a law above all arguments – and they still do – but they were violent and extremely anti-British. Both groups attacked airports and other infrastructure and were successful, being prepared to sustain heavy losses having their members either killed or captured. They had driven a truck full of explosives into the police depot in Tel Aviv, so aggravating the authorities that this triggered the British army to be called in to keep the peace.

We were stationed in a hotel and immediately there was trouble brewing. The population were being screened at the time and, taking up position in a line down the middle of a street, it was our job to stop people moving from one side of the street to the other while the process was carried out. In the afternoon, a throng of people came down a street at right angles to the one we were in and even though the Sergeant tried to stop them, they kept on coming. We were commanded to 'fix bayonets', advance and charge at the crowd. Thankfully they scattered. But I saw a Jewish man beaten up by a British soldier and it made me realise that our side could also perpetrate bad things under stress. This incident would be brushed over, of course. I didn't like it, but I accepted this was the way it had to be if we were to successfully carry out our orders to impose a rule of law.

One evening there was gunfire targeting our hotel. We had to discover who was responsible and I was in one of the two parties of men selected for the task. We had to charge up the stairs of the adjoining blocks of flats, break the doors down if they were closed and lead all the inhabitants out onto the street. I remember smashing a door leading to the roof, looking for stashes of rifles and other munitions, but we didn't find any. This is the closest I came to violent action during my time in the army.

Back in camp, I resumed the life of tedium, relieved only by the small pleasure derived from my little job on the side. I had started up a business as a laundryman, washing and ironing soldiers' clothes for a small fee. I would do the washing in the sinks and plug the iron into the overhead light bulb. I had been taught how to wash and iron by my mother and the lads were quite happy to pass on their laundry to me. They even announced my services on the parade ground. It didn't last long, however, as shortly after my return from Tel Aviv, I received a letter telling me I had been reported to the authorities by the Egyptian laundry company employed to do the washing for the camp. I was told to cease my business activities immediately.

However, there soon arose another opportunity to relive the boredom. I had spotted a notice on the board advertising for people to attend a course to improve 'future prospects' once out of the army. One of these was a painting and decorating course based in an army camp located on the edge of the Suez Canal and built around a series of lakes.

The instructor soon realised that I knew as much as I needed to about painting and decorating and saw an immediate way to put this to his advantage – and as it turned out, mine too. He asked if I would repaint the huge camp map on the gable end of a building, and I was delighted to spend most of my time working by myself. It was hot during the day, and I could swim in the lakes whenever I wanted to cool off.

Something about those swims has stayed with me all my life. During the first part of the day, when I swam before the heat of the sun had taken effect, I noticed that the top layer of the water was cold, while the water underneath was still warm from the sun's heat the day before. This property of water – slow to heat up but retaining its heat for a long time – was new to me but explained why coastal areas have fewer extreme temperatures than, say, cities inland.

It was while painting this gable end and pondering this principle that I received my papers to return to the United Kingdom to be demobbed. I was jubilant. On 28 February 1948, I left the 4th Parachute Regiment, never having parachuted in anger in the service of the army.

We set off for home by ship, and it took ten days to sail from Port Said to Liverpool. I recall standing on the bow of the boat, hour after hour, just watching the wake and the boat rising and falling. It was incredibly tedious, but we occupied ourselves by going to the NAAFI to play table tennis. I didn't read books, but that voyage made me realise that I probably ought to have passed the time this way. On docking in Liverpool, we swapped our khakis for a demob suit and were sent on our way. Similar to many men of my generation, no matter how high the temperature reached in future, I rarely wore shorts again!

I was very happy to leave the army and excited about my future with Lois, who I had already determined I would marry."

Postscript.

A few months later, on 15 May 1948, the mandatory powers Britain had had over much of the Middle East since the end of World War effectively came to an end. The day after the British withdrew from Palestine, David Ben-Gurion, the chairman of the Jewish Agency for Palestine, declared the establishment of the State of Israel. The Arab state armies immediately mobilised, and so began the Arab–Israeli War.

Ironically, units from the Stern Gang and Haganah groups, who had always been condemned by moderate leaders of the Jewish community, were incorporated into the Israeli Defence Force, perfectly illustrating the proverb that *"The enemy of my enemy is perhaps my friend after all."*

Chapter 10: The Conversion

"I was now twenty years old, and my first task following demob was to get a job," Denis recalls.

"Whilst I was away in the army, I had been in touch with the foreman at Harry Robshaw, and while there was never a promise of a job on my return, I hoped that they would take me back on. The foreman, Walter Car, had, in the meantime, left Harry Robshaw to set up his own competitive business. Walter offered me a job immediately on my return home, and I was back in the white overalls within weeks of leaving the army.

The war was over, and I had a job and a girlfriend. Life was good and returned to normal... almost. While I had been away, a major doctrinal split had arisen in the congregation of the Cutsyke Assembly over details enshrined in the doctrine of 'predestination'.

This doctrine tries to explain the paradox between God's omniscience or 'all knowledge' versus man's free will. At the crux of the paradox is the question of whether an individual can himself choose to accept or reject Christ or whether God, because He knows everything, 'leads' a person to take that step of faith, i.e. their salvation is already predestined.

Some of the Cutsyke Assembly were deeply offended by the thought that they didn't have the free will to choose God but to Dad and some others, it was clear that God knew who he would be saving

Dare to be a Daniel

This latter group, which included Dad, Mam, Mr and Mrs. Vernon, Mr Grieves and Denis Holmes, also felt that belief in God's omniscience was such an important part of having a common faith that they decided to leave the Cutsyke Assembly.

This breakaway group proceeded to meet regularly once again in each other's houses, but it wasn't long before they rented new premises and formed their own Castleford Assembly. All of our family went with them.

The rented rooms were situated on Castleford's main shopping street - Carlton Street - and were next door to the Central Methodist Church, where Lois and I would soon be married.

To get to these new premises, you had to walk down a little passage round the back of the shops and proceed up three flights of stairs. There were just two rooms at the top, reminiscent of the upper rooms in which the Last Supper was held on Jesus' last night in Jerusalem before he was crucified.

One room was used for meetings and was furnished very comfortably, with old cinema seats. The other room was a small kitchen, which we would use to serve tea on Sunday afternoons during the 1.5-hour gap before the evening Gospel meeting at 6.30 pm.

Although Dad could only play the organ by ear, he was occasionally called upon to play at these meetings. This gave him some anxiety, and so, feeling that he should try to improve his ability, he started taking piano lessons from a friend. He only managed a few lessons before his teacher dismissed him, telling him, "Dan, I think we should stop these lessons. As soon as I have taught you how to play something properly, you go off and carry on playing by ear!"

Although neither Lois nor I had been converted at this time, we were sympathetic to the scriptures and so would go along to these new Sunday Gospel meetings in support. Lois also carried on teaching at the Sunday School in the Methodist Church.

That same summer, my sister, Hannah, and her husband, Ronnie, employed me to decorate the interior of their house. Whilst I was there, Hannah invited me and Lois to a Rally - a series of Gospel meetings designed to inspire people to join this new religious movement and conducted unusually in a large tent, which it was hoped might appeal to people not used to attending a church service. The tent was pitched in Pontefract, on some spare land opposite the Dunhill factory where the famous liquorish sweets, Pontefract Cakes, are made. We accepted Hannah's invitation and went along.

The tent campaigns were a successful way of recruiting new members to the Brethren movement, and they all took a similar format: prayer meetings were held each night to get the congregation match fit and to request showers of blessing, before a powerful and enthusiastic evangelist would preach. This would happen every night for a fortnight.

The main message of the meetings centred on the truth that we were all born as sinners and how, knowing this, God sacrificed his son to die in order to give us a chance to save ourselves from eternal damnation. Sometimes the story of the crucifixion and the agonies of the cross would be so skilfully described to elicit a sense of gratitude to God for his sacrifice, that you would literally feel as if you were a witness at the scene. On these nights, the tent would be so quiet that you could hear a pin drop.

At the end of each meeting, during the final prayer, it was customary for the preacher to issue a call for anyone to raise their hand if they wanted to take a step of faith and be saved. Those still not persuaded would be reminded that: "There is more joy in heaven over one sinner that repenteth". The organist and choir would then sing the hymn *I Can Hear the Saviour Calling,* in hushed tones as the congregation waited for people to come forward.

Despite the evangelist's best efforts, there was always a shyness that came over everyone to come forward at his appeal - but if the evangelist could get just one or two members of the crowd to break the ice, then others generally followed.

Believers and non-believers alike, everyone enjoyed these campaigns – and at the end of the last meeting on the first week, in the darkness behind my tightly closed eyes, I could sense that Lois had raised her hand. She was led to the front, where one of the elders spoke to her while I waited at the back of the tent. Adam Chambers was the preacher that fortnight, and as Lois and I left the tent, he stopped us at the door and, addressing me, said, 'as her boyfriend, you should think about taking the same step of faith.'

Having had first-hand experience of being raised by a couple who were united in their faith, I knew how marvellous such a unison could be. The preacher was gently reminding me that the two of us would begin heading down different paths if I didn't take the same step of faith. On the long walk home to Lois' house on Ashton Road, she confirmed she had made that step and had given her life to Christ. I wasn't surprised. I was also able to explain what would now be expected of her, already being familiar with the rites and rituals of Assembly life. But by reminding her, I started to think about what this meant for my life ahead too.

> *And there it was, I did it. I took a decision of faith. No stars, No trumpets. Just a decision.*

The rally with the tent moved to Featherstone for the second week of meetings. The theme in the first week had been *From Eden to Calvary* and in the second week continued to *From Calvary to Glory*. Adam Chambers' preaching had been so gripping in that first week that Lois and I continued to attend.

Sometime after the rally, Hannah and Ronnie invited us over to tea. At the end of the evening, Ronnie suggested he close the evening by saying a word of prayer. I had spent the past few weeks considering my life so far, contrasting the comfort of my family life in the Brethren to the world experience the army had provided me. had given a lot of thought to what the preacher had said at the rally and during Ronnie's prayer, I came to a decision in my heart. Without saying anything, I admitted I was a sinner and guilty before God.

accepted I needed a saviour, and I believed that it was Jesus who had paid for my sin by dying on the cross. This decision, once made, was immutable. And there it was; I did it. I took a decision of faith. No stars, no trumpets. Just a decision.

As I walked Lois home that night, I told her my news, and she was very happy. Then I made my way down Flass Lane towards home. It was harvest time, and as I walked alongside one of the wonderful fields of harvested corn, I impulsively knelt beside a stook of corn and prayed. I thanked God for showing me the way of salvation, and the enormity of my decision was not lost on me.

The next morning, I rose early to tell my father, as I knew he would be very pleased about my conversion. I found him in the pig sty. However, to my disappointment, his reaction was not as enthusiastic as I had hoped. Instead, he replied, 'Well lad, we'll see how tha goes on!' Such was Dad's nature.

Shortly afterwards, abiding by God's word, Lois and I were both baptised at Featherstone Gospel Hall where my father had been baptised. At the front of the hall, underneath the pulpit, they had installed an enormous bath, semi-submerged into the floor, with three or four steps at one end leading down into it. This was where baptisms of 'full immersion' took place.

It was easy enough to fill the enormous bath with water using a hosepipe. The difficult part was getting the water to be warm enough to avoid the impact of the temperature distracting participants from the seriousness of the occasion. Heating this volume of water using an electrical element was rather inexact, so it generally commenced a day or so before the ceremony. With this amount of effort required to heat the baptismal bath, it was customary to wait until there was as big a group as possible volunteering for the experience.

Our baptism took place on a Sunday evening as part of the Gospel service, and friends and family were invited to see this public declaration of our belief in God. As explained in *Romans* 6:3-6, going under the water represents the death and burial of Jesus Christ as well as the death of our old self. Being brought out of the water symbolises Christ's resurrection and our subsequent rebirth as one of his disciples.

These baptism ceremonies were very exciting. Nervous participants changed in separate rooms; the chaps in the cellar and the ladies in a room upstairs. Each one donned their swimming togs and then struggled into dark blue, heavy sack-like garments, with elastic at the neck and arms. At the appointed time, the congregation would gather around the bath (kids at the front) as each candidate would make their way down the steps, one at a time.

The candidates would be greeted in the water by one of the elders who, waist deep, would stand beside them and hold them by clasping both their hands in front with his left hand, stretching his right arm around their back. The elder would proceed to ask each candidate to confess that '[they] believed in the Lord Jesus Christ and [they would] commit to following him as [their] saviour.' Once the candidate had responded in the affirmative, the elder would lower them backwards into the water and then, as quickly as possible, hoist them back out before the sodden weight of the baptismal gown threatened to pin them both fatally to the bottom of the bath. It wasn't an easy job, as the candidate was helpless to assist in the process, but the successful resurrection of each candidate was rewarded with an uproarious chorus from the congregation of the hymn *Up from The Grave He Arose*.

Lois and I were very happy together, and our joint commitment to a Christian life had laid the foundation that sealed our union for 73 years of married life ahead. At the tender ages of twenty-one and nineteen, we decided to marry and start a family as soon as we could."

Dare to be a Daniel

Denis and Lois marry on January 1st, 1949.

Chapter 11: Fishing For Souls

"Once we were baptised, we were considered full members of the Assembly and could therefore take part in Breaking of Bread. Lois and I were very content with our new life, and I had peace knowing that God had promised to take care of me and my family if He was in all of the decisions that we made. Our lives had now changed, and we began to observe the tenets of Christianity as best we could.

Our spiritual aim over the years was to be more and more like Christ, and reading the scriptures was the best way to achieve a deeper understanding of him. As the apostle Paul taught the early Christians, we were baby Christians, and the Bible was our food. First, we fed on 'milk' to understand simple principles, but as we reached spiritual maturity, we fed on 'meat', representing more complex spiritual doctrines.

> *Lois and I faithfully read a chapter of the Bible in the morning and another at the end of the day...Over the years, we must have read the Bible cover to cover over forty times!*

Lois and I faithfully read a chapter of the Bible every morning and another at the end of each day, beginning with the *New Testament*. Over the years, we might have read the Bible, cover-to-cover, over forty times! Granted, we habitually skipped the books of *Kings and Chronicles*, as they tended to deal with genealogy in the kingdoms of

Israel and Judah. Instead, we more often reread our top two favourite books of the Bible - *Hebrews* and *Romans*.

Hebrews was a particular favourite because it lays out Christ's teachings very clearly, and how they apply to the life of a believer. *Romans,* on the other hand, tells us all about God, who He is and what He has done. It tells us what Jesus' death accomplished and, importantly, what we were like without Christ and who we are after trusting in Christ.

Unusually for some married couples, we started our married life knowing that God had the primary place in our lives and that everything we did thereafter was to be first and foremost for his glory.

Initially, we lived with Alf and Mona in their two-up-two-down, with our new baby, Christine. But it wasn't long before I had earned enough money to take out a mortgage on a small new build in Pontefract - No I, Kingsway. Despite it being adjacent to another muck stack, we loved living there. There were farmers' fields in the vicinity, and, best of all, we had some wonderful neighbours who became lifelong friends. However, the first of life's challenges was about to land.

After only seven months working for Car & Co, the seasonality of the work meant that I was made redundant. This came as a shock, but part-time work was available, and I got on with accepting the odd decorating job. One day, I was in the paint supplies shop in Castleford when I ran into an ex-colleague from Walter Car. He told me that JL

Rodgers was hiring painters and decorators and that, best of all, their offices were just on the other side of the road from the shop. I immediately went across to enquire.

I spoke to a Mr John Dickinson, who confirmed that JL Rodgers was hiring but on two conditions. First, the painter and decorator had to be qualified. Second, they had to live in Pontefract, as the company didn't want to incur travel expenses. Since I qualified on both counts, I was given the job as a full-time painter at Pontefract Barracks. I started on the following Monday and, to my further delight, it being Winter, it was an inside job.

Shortly after I had started there, JL Rodgers folded, and I was informed that it had been bought by a joinery company – Poskitt of Airedale. I didn't know it then, but I was to remain with this company for the rest of my working life.

Sharing the good news of the gospel isn't simply a suggestion; it's a command that Jesus sets out for us. And so, in the Castleford Assembly, we sought to do the same: we would go 'fishing for souls'. We loved to see others brought into the same fellowship through our evangelical work, and my very first open-air evangelism took the form of standing outside our Assembly premises in Carlton Street.

Our church service took place on Sundays, which was also the day that the cinemas and theatres in Castleford were shut. As a result, the young people of the town would spend the day doing a duck walk along Carlton Street, Bridge Street, and Church Street - a heaven-sent shoal of fish waiting to be baited with a soul-searching question such as 'do you know where you will spend eternity?' Yet, despite this rich source of sinners, we felt that we weren't able to reach many people from our discreet premises, and so we began to think about alternative ways we could spread the Gospel and increase our fellowship.

It was the summer of 1952, and I was twenty-four years old with a wife and child and a second baby on the way. I was enjoying life. We decided to hold another tent campaign, this time with children's meetings in the morning and adult meetings in the evening. Hiring a similar marquee to the one where Lois was converted, we sited it this time in Austin Road, Airedale - a large suburb of Castleford that housed a huge new council estate. The response to the children's meetings, in particular, was outstanding, and I felt I was being called by God to continue to work with children after the campaign ended. After discussing this with the elders of the Assembly in Castleford, they gave me permission to set about finding a more permanent premises for children's work in Airedale."

Dare to be a Daniel

Chapter 12: Prizes and Surprises

"After much searching on the streets of Airedale on my bicycle, I came across an old wooden hut in Royds Avenue that was built by the colliery but was currently being used by the Unemployment Association for recreational activities. It had a license to sell cigarettes, and it was the profits from this that funded their activities. In reality, it was used mainly by elderly people for somewhere to sit and spend the evening, and so they readily agreed to let us use the hut on Sunday mornings in exchange for a small rent.

Inside, the hut had a very simple layout: one huge room with toilets at the back. The room could be divided into two with a huge, dark red, floor-to-ceiling velvet curtain. This would be great for separating the room for Sunday School classes. There was an open coal fire at one end of the room, but the main heat came from two six-inch diameter pipes that ran down one side of the hut. These pipes were heated by a coal-fired boiler which was situated in a little lean-to shed at the side of the hut.

It had everything we needed, and in October 1954, we opened the first Airedale Sunday School, to be run every Sunday at 11 am.

Each Sunday morning, I would cycle the 3 miles from our house in Pontefract to light the boiler and the coal fire ready for the meeting. Lois would walk there with the children (after putting the beef brisket into the oven on a low heat) as we didn't have a car, and it was too

Dare to be a Daniel

early for the Sunday bus service. We kept up this routine for many years until I finally got a car nearly seventeen years later, in 1971. By then, we had four children and the walking posse had grown during that time to include other kids from the estate, and a friend of ours, Mr. Fryer, eventually took pity on Lois and regularly gave her and the children a lift. But I continued to cycle all that time.

I was the Superintendent of the Sunday School, and we recruited some good teachers from the Castleford Assembly: Ronnie Smith, Joe and Ethel Martin, Geoff Robinson and Len Brook, among others. After extensive leafleting in the surrounding streets and at the local primary schools, our school took off spectacularly. It started with thirty children and soon reached fifty as word spread further. At times, attendance could swell to one-hundred, but reliably remained above forty for many years. It was something new and wasn't against the will of their parents at that time.

> *Children would be transfixed as they were transported back to biblical times.*

One family who had a particularly big influence on the Sunday School, back then and to this day, as trustees of the Assembly, was the Hull Family. They had five children – Jean, Denise, Jacqueline, Robert, and Arthur, and all five participated as they reached Sunday School age. They were just one of many families who we came to know over the years, many growing up to become members of the Assembly.

The Sunday School service was always exciting. I discovered a gift for teaching children and always knew how to bring out the fun in the kids while also keeping a lid on their boisterousness. As well as chorus singing and story-telling, there were games to play and Bible verses to learn. I even decided to try to teach the children to recite all sixty-six books of the Bible! Ambitious, you might think, but I came up with an effective technique to make it easy to learn the verses by setting them to a rhythm. With the quick minds of children, they had soon learnt them all by heart, and there is very probably a large number of people of advanced years in Airedale today whose party piece is to recite the names of all sixty-six books!

I also employed a compelling story-telling technique of looking down the end of a roll of wallpaper as if it were a telescope – or 'Biblescope', as I called it. I would pretend my Biblescope was looking back in time and was watching a Bible event unfold. Children would be transfixed as they were transported back to biblical times.

During the summer, we would also hold a series of open-air children's meetings. We called these meetings '6.30 Specials' or 'Sunshine Corners'. Prior to each one, I would walk around the streets with a tannoy calling all children to come along, promising 'prizes and surprises!' We would sit the children down on a patch of grass, and then the teaching and fun would begin.

I never underestimated the effectiveness of an incentive, and I would make various-sized tickets from wallpaper worth differing amounts of points. If kids sat up straight, sang well, or successfully

Dare to be a Daniel

learned the Bible verse, they would earn points. Then, at the end, they would queue up to exchange their tickets for prizes of sweets, where they would be encouraged to come to Sunday School each week.

The Sunday School year ended with a prize-giving, which would take the form of a creative but entertainingly under-rehearsed play involving sets, props, costumes, sketches, and singing. One play involved using our own row boat 'Daniel' rigged up to illustrate the perils of being tossed about on the storms of life.

Eventually, we formed a Youth Group for older Sunday School children who, in turn, formed a football team, playing other teams such as one from Cutsyke Gospel Hall on a pitch at the top of Queen's Park. We'd play on Saturday afternoons and sometimes mid-week. On one occasion, the team asked me to be the ref. I wasn't as familiar with the rules of the game as I had thought, and my lack of knowledge was soon exposed, resulting in quite cries of: 'Hey Mr. Noon, did you see what he did! Mr. Noooooon?!'

Whilst there never a shortage of children attending the Sunday School, occasional efforts would be made to bolster numbers. One of the most successful recruitment initiatives was the one inspired by finding a pile of old 45-inch records that no one wanted. I announced the new challenge, called 'Beat the Record', at the very next meeting. The idea was that we would count all the children in attendance and chalk the total on one of the records. We would then hang that record on a nail in the wall until the following week, when we would recount the attendees. If the number of children exceeded the previous week' attendees, the record was beaten and would be replaced by a new record with the new, higher number chalked on it. This is the part where it got exciting.

One lucky child would be chosen to come to the front, where I would kneel down and proffer my bare head for the child to smash the record over. Being made of brittle shellac, the old 45" would shatter satisfyingly on impact – much to the utter delight of the children. To enhance the glee of the ceremony further, I would feign abject fear and pain, though also with the occasional non-feigned cut forehead. The following Sunday, you could absolutely rely on the children to have told all their friends about this wonderful challenge and numbers would soar week after week.

However, utilising God's word – which is 'quick and powerful and sharper than any two-edged sword' (*Hebrews*, Ch 4 v 12), tent campaigns were always the best way of encouraging new recruits to Sunday School over the years. One of the most memorable was one run during the 1970s by a wonderful saviour-of-souls called George Tryon. He owned a caravan and would move around the country, leading tent campaigns with amazing fervour, enthusiasm, and success. He also had the stature of a giant, and his stock joke was that, while most people referred to their body as a temple, his was more like a block of flats.

In 1960, due to the success of the Sunday School, there was enough interest from adults - including parents of the Sunday school children - to form a new Assembly in Airedale. The old hut was duly purchased for £150, and a new sign put over the door, 'Airedale Gospel Hall'.

On that first Sunday, we had seven people breaking bread alongside Lois and I - Mr and Mrs Robinson, Mr and Mrs Brooks, Ivy Greaves, Mrs Webster, and Mr Willy Reynolds. A vigorous schedule of Sunday meetings was agreed upon, which, remarkably, has remained largely unchanged in the last 70 years. The day begins with Sunday School at 11 am, followed by Breaking of Bread at 3 pm, and ends with the Gospel Service at 6.30 pm. Bible study then takes place every Thursday evening.

In all respects, our Sunday was the most demanding day of the week. After Sunday School, we would catch the bus home, where we would be greeted by the smell of Sunday dinner. For decades, this meal consisted of a starter of two scone-sized Yorkshire puddings served with onion gravy, followed by boiled beef brisket (having spent three hours on a low heat in the oven) accompanied by more Yorkshire puddings. Pudding, in the sense of dessert, was a treacle sponge with custard. But if there were any Yorkshire puddings remaining after pudding...we would eat them cold, spread with butter, and a sprinkling of caster sugar. As you can tell, we absolutely loved our Yorkshire pudding!

With all that polished off, we would catch the bus back to Airedale in time for Breaking of Bread. This communion meeting was for Assembly members, members by virtue of being baptised. The cohort would then stay around for a 'fellowship tea' - by which it was meant that everyone would bring food and share it together - before the main evangelical Gospel service commenced at 6.30 pm. We made use of the time before the Gospel Service to take the word onto the streets in open-air meetings or by giving out tracts. I absolutely love open-air work. If others came up with an idea for spreading the Gospel, I would always have the courage to put it into practice."

Ruth

Dare to be a Daniel

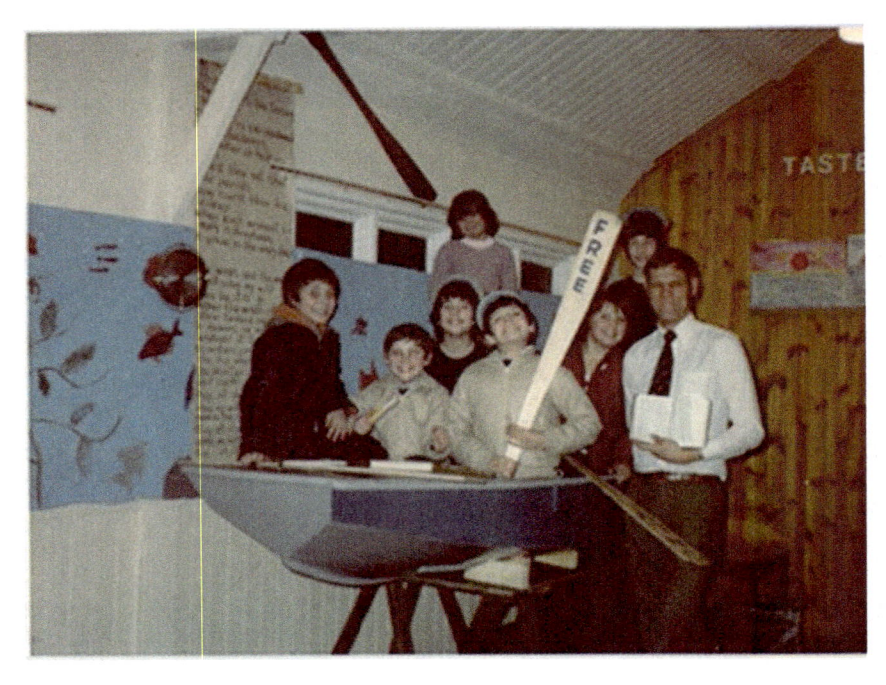

Airedale Assembly 1950s. Sunday School prize giving with Harry

Yorkshire Sunday School Camp, Ingleton, 1960s

Chapter 13: The Yorkshire Sunday School Camp

"The highlight of the Sunday School year for the children of Airedale, and indeed all over Yorkshire, was the Yorkshire Sunday School camp. The camp was started by brethren from the Ossett Assembly - Mr. Glam, Mr. J Watts, and Mr. L Waterhouse - in the 1940s, and Lois and I were involved very early on in its organisation. Every Whitsuntide, Sunday School children who had paid a small amount each week to fund it, were taken by coach to a delightful spot in Ingleton, high in the Yorkshire Dales on a hillside above Beezley Farm, which was owned by an arable sheep farmer called Mr. Chapman. He had a public path that went by the end of the field we occupied, where he sold us and passers-by delicious milkshakes using his cows' fresh milk.

We took the coach to the village and walked up the road to the camp, looking at the shadows cast by sweeping clouds and listening to the sound of curlews. An advance party had arrived the week before with an open-backed lorry to pitch some leaky ex-army tents. The tents were capable of sleeping twelve children and their leaders. In the early days, there were just six tents and fifty children. This quickly grew to two hundred children from Assemblies as far away as Hull and Scotland.

Dare to be a Daniel

The advance party would also dig a row of 'dry' toilets, which consisted of a six-foot trench over which a shed was placed containing rudimentary cubicles with benches with a hole in them. A distinctly non-coveted task was to help fill in the lively trench after camp.

> *A distinctly non-coveted task was to help fill in the 'dry holes' (toilets) after camp*

The daily camp schedule consisted of breakfast served from a small wooden hut, followed by a tent meeting in the large marquee, which would be filled with wooden benches. Lights and a microphone were powered by a noisy generator. The service was led by Dennis Gibson with a piano accordion led by Jonny Watts and accompanied by hearty singing from the Camp Chorus Book. Testimonies (the story of individual conversions) were given, and energetic preaching was delivered by the most promising young members of the congregation.

At the start of the camp, children and adults alike were divided into four team colours for a week-long competition with cups and a wooden spoon at stake. Points were gained (or lost) for your house if you excelled at various activities. There was even an award for 'Camp Comic'! It evoked a wonderful team spirit amongst camp members.

The first points of the day were earned from a tent inspection, which took place whilst everyone attended the first meeting. The results of this cleanliness and tidiness check were announced by the 'Camp Policeman' at the end of each morning's meeting, with excitement reigning throughout the week as to which team was winning the Camp House competition. Every activity elicited chances to earn house points, including spud-bashing. A call for this would be broadcast over the tannoy: 'Volunteers required to help remove the eyes from tonight's spuds – so they can't see where they're going!'

The first meeting of the day would be followed by quiet time, where the tent leader and their assistant were expected to be on hand to provide spiritual guidance. The aim of the camp, after all, was to point children to the saviour of souls and the warmth of Christian fellowship.

The rest of the day would be filled with good-humoured field sports, such as 'marrieds versus singles' football, rounders, and tug-of-war, as well as games and arts and crafts activities. Every Wednesday afternoon was taken up with the challenge to climb Mount Ingleborough, led by Mr. Lamb, the 'Sports Master', who would sing motivational choruses along the way. When the camp moved to larger premises elsewhere, this event was replaced with an exciting 'It's a Knockout' afternoon with team mascots that were enthusiastically made in the creative activities tent for more house points.

In the evenings, everyone would come together for the evening rally, where a singing competition called 'Top Town' would take place between Sunday Schools. Airedale Sunday School entered every year and even won it on one occasion. Performances included comic sketches, such as 'Gladys and Enid' featuring a brother and sister who brought the house down, and more young people singing their hearts out. The last hours of the day were then occupied in the

Dare to be a Daniel

senior and junior coffee bars, where films were shown, and discussions had that would forge many lasting romances, friendships and lives dedicated to the Saviour.

Over time, there evolved a camp band, bookshop, coffee shop, bank and hospital, and even a Camp Radio (qualifications were having a good stock of 78s), all provided by enthusiastic helpers. But arguably the most vital role of the camp was the camp cook. For many years, that role was held by Brian Holmes, presiding over cooking facilities in a large tent with no running water, which meant that water had to be hauled out of the river and trundled in a large tank by cart up to the camp site.

> *Lifters, Diggers, Pushers, Pullers, Grafters, Shifters. No experience required, full training given. If you can't be involved physically, please pray for God's blessing.*

Each day, Brian planned a simple but hearty menu, always starting with 'quick-set' porridge for breakfast and one glorious night of chips! Yet, despite these culinary feats, the cookhouse was the gentle brunt of camp jokes. Even the Camp Nurse would report in the meetings that there had been no insect bites, no broken limbs, and no other serious life-changing injuries sustained by the camp food that day!

The washing of bodies and clothes was done in the chillingly cold water of the nearby river, which had stepping stones across. It must have raised the eyebrows of many a hillwalker during the 1950s and

'60s to witness the hurried ablutions of semi-attired bathers. The river was also made good use of for full immersion baptisms as professions of faith were made during camp week.

These Sunday School camps provided many treasured memories but as there were tapes of the evening rallies were for sale and a newsletter, *Fragments*, circulated four times a year, it never seemed long until the next camp was around the corner and the call made for:

"'Lifters, Diggers, Pushers, Pullers, Grafters, Shifters. No experience required, full training given. If you can't be involved physically, please pray for God's blessing on this wonderful work.'

…and it would all begin again."

Camp reached a peak of four hundred children in the 1990s and to this day continues to play an important role in recruiting members to the Brethren assemblies under its new name, The Yorkshire Christian Camp (yorkshirechristiancamp.co.uk)."

Dare to be a Daniel

Gathering for a baptism by the river.

Competing for house points in a tug of war

Dare to be a Daniel

Messing about in the river where they washed every morning

Dare to be a Daniel

Putting the finishing touch to the new Gospel Hall.

And in full 1980s colour.

Chapter 14: Take it as Gospel - Building a New Gospel Hall

"Back in Airedale, the old hall was already shabby and had been further scarred by a fire that had ripped through the place after an ember from the coal fire escaped and set alight the heavy velvet curtain that divided the hall into two. The freehold and the hut had been purchased long ago.

But the opportunity to build a new Gospel Hall soon came when three wooden buildings conveniently sited just up the road from the old hall, came up for sale:

They were previously used by the Anglican church and most recently used by the local Catholic church for services. It was therefore fitting that they were now destined to be acquired by the evangelicals. The largest hut was in good condition, and we were offered it at a good price on the condition that we cleared away the other two huts.

We managed to fund the purchase ourselves and also received a generous donation from the enormous family-owned construction firm, John Laing. John Laing himself was in the Brethren Assembly, so our request to his charitable trust fell on sympathetic ears. The call then went out to our local Assemblies for volunteers to help with the various trades we needed. And so, in the winter of 1980, a small group of committed Christians turned up on evenings and Saturdays, week after week, to help. We began by dismantling all three huts. The smallest hut was carried across the road and rebuilt next to our hall. This was then used to store the second hut (saved only for spare timber) and the third hut which we intended to re-erect.

The building work itself commenced in the spring. The walls of our new hut were built in 12ft sections. We came up with a very simple design consisting of an oblong of six sections long by two sections wide. This oblong would be partitioned into four parts. The first part had a central lobby with toilets and cloakrooms on either side. Then came the main room, made up of three sections, followed by two further parts housing a large room and a kitchen.

Fortunately, there was enough room behind our old hut to build this back part first. This meant our services could continue until we had built the back part. Then we held our meetings in the back part whilst we built the front end and knocked through to join the two buildings together. The hall was finished with the old asbestos roof and a new brick skin was built around the entire perimeter of the building to ensure it endured into the next century.

> *Inside, as per the Brethren way, there were no religious emblems, crosses or stained-glass windows. Instead, just a simple text on the front wall above the pulpit.*

During the process, we were fortunate to find a valuable source of expertise in a retired miner who lived directly opposite the Gospel

Hall and, having seen what was going on, offered his help. He was on hand throughout the entire project and was only ever a few yards away when needed. There was also never a shortage of volunteers to undertake the hard labour either and, apart from the bricklayer and electricians, all the work was completed by keen amateurs.

Inside, as per the Brethren way, there were no religious emblems, crosses, or stained-glass windows. Instead, a simple text on the front wall above the pulpit - which had been reclaimed from another church – read: 'Taste and see that the Lord is good' (*Psalm* 34:8).

The completion of the building was featured in the local Pontefract and Castleford Express and marked with a campaign of Gospel meetings. However, the local youths weren't so appreciative of our smart new building, and over the years, I've defended the premises against broken windows, break-ins, and stone-throwing during the Gospel Service. My vandal-defence routine for decades has been to stand at the back of the Hall during each service, ready to greet any latecomers - but also best placed to creep out and chase off any stone-throwing miscreants."

Dare to be a Daniel

A Christmas party in the Gospel Hall

Chapter 15: Daytrips and Jaunts

As Denis's youngest daughter, I take up the story recalling a childhood in the 1970's and '80s spent learning to expect the unexpected...

Dad retains his boyish delight from the fun and adventures of his youth. He was always excitedly looking for the next outreach idea that might bring new people to Christ. It was okay to borrow an idea from a secular source, but every activity had to, first and foremost, glorify Christ.

In the '60s and '70s, a trend began for Working Men's Clubs to reward their loyal customers with an annual coach trip to the seaside for them and their families, which usually included a voucher for free fish and chips. These trips quickly gained huge popularity, and clubs would compete for the best destinations and incentives to offer their customers. On one occasion, fourteen coaches were chartered by the Magnet Pub in Airedale for a seaside trip.

Dad could see the appeal of these trips and decided to lay on a similar outing each summer for loyal Sunday School children and their parents. These occasions soon became a hit and were much looked forward to. The destinations began with low-key settings such as a park in Halifax or Purston, but as the popularity grew, the locations became more ambitious. Bolton Abbey was particularly memorable, if it wasn't for the fact that our visit awkwardly coincided

Dare to be a Daniel

with the performing of a 'Druid Fertility Ritual', which, naturally, we were all discouraged from watching! There were also several visits to Ilkley Moor, which included a challenge at the end of the day to climb the two rocks, whose names 'The Cow and Calf', jokingly underestimates their size.

The day of these outings would commence early, with the ladies of the Assembly gathered in the back room of the Gospel Hall, making a picnic lunch (eaten in the Yorkshire way, strictly at mid-day). Egg sandwiches were a firm favourite on these outings. Once the bread was buttered and filled, the sandwiches were piled carefully back inside the bread bags. Then there were tins and tins of buns, all made from the recipe from the Be-Ro Flour cookbook and topped with coloured icing or buttercream, which were all added to a rather apologetic pile of fruit.

The coaches would arrive promptly at 10 am to the excited cries of "they're here, they're here," and we would proceed to load everything into the luggage compartment along with a water boiler - retired with distinction after boiling the last of the Noon children's nappies - and huge kettles for making tea. Everyone mucked in to load up the coaches, and then we were off. The chorus singing would always start fairly soon after we were underway. Amongst the favourites were the ones with accompanying actions, such as 'Deep and Wide':

Deep and wide, deep and wide,

There's a fountain flowing deep and wide

Plunge right in, lose your sin,

There's a fountain flowing deep and wide

On arrival at the destination, the trip would always follow the same format. We would set up camp and get the boiler going (as it took several hours to boil), and then the races would start. There were all sorts of races to get stuck into; sack race, egg, and spoon, relay, fathers' race, mothers', etc. Then it would all end with a rounders match and a hugely entertaining tug of war before dinner was served, which we would munch sitting on the grass.

After free time in the afternoon splashing in a river or the sea, coachloads of weary kids would wend their way home, only to bounce back to Sunday School the following morning.

While a lot of the outreach activities were aimed at children, the adults were always catered for with social gatherings in the Hall, which would end with a short Gospel talk. One of these gatherings aimed at the elderly and which ran for years was the 'Pea and Pie Supper'. This was exactly as described: an evening of entertainment and games, topped off with a meal of meat pie, mashed potato, and mushy peas.

Though the name of the event implies the pea was the main attraction, it was the pie that was the hero. A delicious puff pastry beef pie served with gravy to soak through the buttery mashed potato and perfectly accompanied with a side serving of overnight-soaked mushy peas. The smell of these delicious pies warming in the oven in the back of the Gospel Hall would permeate through the preceding entertainment until the meal was eventually served to a pie-frenzied audience of thirty or so pensioners.

> *Although the name of the event implies the pea was the main attraction, it was the pie that was the hero*

The attendees of these gatherings were largely recruited through handwritten leaflets pushed through doors in the locality, though Dad would often knock on the doors to give a personal invite. On one of these occasions, the door was opened by an elderly lady in her slippers who said 'yes'. She would love to come to the Pea and Pie Supper, so long as Dad (for some curious reason) "didn't tell her daughter". He agreed to pick her up on the appointed day. Which he did. When she opened the door, Dad had to remind her about her commitment to come to the event, but she needed no further persuasion and readily agreed to come at once, as long as Dad kept his side of the bargain not to tell her daughter. She was so keen to come, in fact, that she forgot to change out of her slippers as she left the house!

The evening went along the usual lines of recitations, puzzles, and sketches, rounded off by the pea and pie supper and a talk. However as the meal ended, this lady stood up in her slippers and said she wanted to sing a song. As she did so, everyone remarked what a beautiful voice she had.

At the end of the evening, as was the norm, Dad provided lifts home - but Dad got quite a surprise when he pulled into this lady's street to see a blue flashing light outside her house. Realising that the daughter had reported her missing mother to the police, he quickly got the lady out of the car and steered her surreptitiously up the pathway. Feeling his duty was done, he decided he didn't have to be brave enough to face questioning from the police and the anxious daughter as to why her mother had been missing for several hours – while still wearing her slippers – and left them to it.

Despite ensuring an itinerary of events catering to all ages, many of Dad's religious activities were aimed at children. He is relentlessly cheerful around children and loves being silly and joining in games to this day. He also loves an outing, a ramble, or an adventure and was easily persuaded to do any or all of them.

The group outings were made possible due to Dad's work success. He had long before been made manager of the painting and decorating arm of Poskitt Pallets Ltd and given a company car (always a Ford Cortina), which was essential for measuring-up jobs and for site visits. He was given a new one every couple of years and his first job was always to refit his home-made roof rack to the roof. Even more essential to the facilitation of Dad's Assembly activities, however, was the full use he was given of the Poskitt van. During the working week, this vehicle was used for the transportation of painting personnel to and from jobs, but come the evenings and weekends, the van became pivotal to the smooth running of Dad's evangelical outreach work and was perfect for transporting children back and forth on outings.

Given the aging profile of the congregation, it was also useful for ferrying people who didn't have their own transport – quietly setting aside the van's actual purpose. It was a large transit van and, inside, had two wooden benches fitted on either side, which were perfect to sit on and could house about twelve passengers (young and old) at a time. Fortuitously, there were no windows in the back section, as the police may have had reason to object to Dad's unusual cargo. It never occurred to Dad at the time that he was committing an offence, and so, in this way, many hundreds of kids and adults, masquerading as Poskitt's Painting and Decorating professionals, were ferried to and from outings over the years. The van passed unnoticed and was driven without incident throughout.

> *Fortuitously, there were no windows in the back section, as the police may have had reason to object to Dad's unusual cargo.*

The outings themselves included memorable day trips to the likes of Brimham Rocks, where children would be let loose to charge around on the lunar-like landscape, happily chasing, hiding and losing themselves in the moment.

Dare to be a Daniel

For us kids, it was like having a minibus permanently on hand. We could always take as many friends along where ever we went. The swimming baths were a regular destination on these outings, and Dad could never wait to use his somewhat superior lung capacity to play dead in the water, floating motionlessly to the increasing concern of young spectators, who would at first be delighted and then panic-stricken as they desperately tried to turn him over to a face-up breathing position.

Dad is always utterly selfless in giving his time to others. Things didn't necessarily have to have a Christian motive either, as long as they helped others out and were, of course, morally sound. That said, one activity that came close to the moral line was when the Youth Group asked whether he could take them to Bradford Ice Rink on Friday nights, which was disco night. The Youth Group loved it: kids their own age, disco lights, darkness, and very loud pop music. Dad would patiently wait it out, gliding around the rink for hours, alone with his arms tucked behind his back like a stately galleon, just tolerating the loud disco music. Where he had learned to skate is anyone's guess, but we teenagers never seem to improve from either circling the perimeter rail with a vice-like grip or flailing like clowns in the middle until we hit the deck. For the teens, however, it was worth it for the occasional stop for a snog in the tradesman's tunnel (nicknamed the 'Tunnel of Love') halfway 'round the rink. Nonetheless, Dad took us ice skating until the novelty wore off for the group, not him.

Dare to be a Daniel

More to Dad's liking was our regular trip "TO THE WOODS!" When Dad would shout this phrase at the top of his voice and raise both arms above his head, we all knew we were in for a treat. We would gather anyone who was around, including any kids in the street, pile in the back of the van, and make our way to a beautiful valley spot called Wentbridge Woods.

The routine was always the same: park the van on the grass verge at the top of the hill; pelt down the hill; ramble through the woods to the stepping stones over the beck, try not to fall in; and then run across the fields at the other side where eventually Dad would follow behind carrying a rope over his shoulder. He would then proceed to throw the rope twice around the top branch of a tree and slot a bit of wood (stashed behind the same tree for next time) into the loop to form a swing. This left a long end to the rope dangling to pull the swing back and forth. Each child would then take turns to be swung until they had had enough, and we would all begin the walk back to the van via another route and a bridge over the beck. Bliss for the children - and no sight or sound of health & safety!

Another group outing that the Poskitt van made possible was the Lyke Wake Walk. This challenge entailed a 40-mile trek from Osmotherley across the beautiful but relentless North Yorkshire Moors, ending on the coast of the North Sea at Ravenscar. It's pretty boring terrain, but the end of the walk rewards with a view of the sea. The walk must be completed in 24hrs so, to prevent walking in the dark at the end of the trek, most people start at midnight and aim to finish around late afternoon. Dad had completed this challenge several times already with family, and so he could not resist sharing his enthusiasm for the challenge each time by inviting either a neighbour or someone from the Gospel Hall to join in. It was, after all, a great thing to be able to complete, and there was always room for another in the van.

However, Dad's enthusiasm to share was always infectious but sometimes misplaced. He decided to take some of the younger adults from the Youth Group on this challenge. A bunch of more ill-equipped teenagers has rarely been seen. None of them had proper footwear (one wore sandals!), one turned up with no food, and most had insufficient waterproof clothing. Defeated, Dad arrived back with them all by mid-morning - within hours of setting off - as they had protested too much at being hungry, blistered, and wet. Still there would always be another outing!

Dare to be a Daniel

Poskitt Painter's van. 'Use the professionals'

Dare to be a Daniel

1980s Sunday School cohort

Dare to be a Daniel

Preaching in Castleford town centre

Chapter 16: God's Great Commission

As he was about to ascend into Heaven, Jesus exhorted his followers to: "Go ye therefore and teach all nations" (*Matthew*, 28:18). Dad took this commission as authority to tell everyone about Jesus.

Dad's zeal to obey this commandment is rocket-fuelled by the knowledge that "the harvest is plentiful, but the labourers are few". In practice, he is ready to take the opportunity to share his experience of Christ with everyone he meets.

In the '70s and '80s, it was policy to pick up hitchhikers on long car journeys, and there was no shortage of people sticking out their thumbs by the roadside in those days. Dad was never put off by the fact we already had four people in the Cortina and the only spare seat was in the back, between me and my sister! The hitcher would inevitably engage the family in cheerful chat whilst we all waited for what we knew was coming. Soon enough, Dad would pose his inevitable leading question to the unsuspecting passenger; something along the lines of, "What role does faith play in your life?" This would render the rest of us silent for the remainder of the trip while we witnessed, with sympathy, the hitcher wriggling on the hook of Dad's extemporising. I wonder how many of these hitchers decided after one of these journeys that this free method of travel really wasn't worth it, after all.

Dare to be a Daniel

Dad would confess years later that there were occasions where he preferred not to share his love of God - to my memory, they were infrequent - as he would feel ashamed afterwards that he hadn't been a good servant of the Lord.

People in need have often sought Dad's help (and no, I'm not referring to the burglar who entered my parent's bedroom looking for the 'collection box'! He underestimated this para's army training as he fled, only to be caught in pursuit by a cool-as-cucumber, pyjama-clad man). However, he is well aware of the potential folly of giving people money, preferring instead to provide a means of 'earning' it. His go-to idea to help those without a job was to purchase a ladder, bucket, and a shammy leather to equip the needy person to start a window-cleaning round. I'm not sure the recipients were so grateful.

One such recipient was Harry, a local resident. Harry looked scary. In fact, he had the looks and build of Frankenstein: over six feet tall with his face a strange linen grey colour. His voice was hoarse from years of smoking, and his fingers tinged nicotine yellow. He also suffered from epilepsy, which, to be fair, did greatly impede his success in getting a job. As such, he never had any money. Dad decided to provide him with his special window-cleaning starter pack. However, Harry sold the ladder and, still desperate for money, called the police to say he had been burgled and the money from his gas meter had been stolen. The police made enquiries at Harry's neighbours' house to see whether they had heard anything suspicious the previous night. Their reply: "We didn't hear anything over the

Dare to be a Daniel

noise of Harry knocking the living daylights out of his gas meter!" That was Harry - the incorrigible rogue whose memory still lives on in every family Christmas game of 'Who am I?'

Mum was similarly imbued with boundless generosity, living by the Bible truth that "if any man will sue thee, and take away thy coat, let him have thy cloak also". (*Matthew 5:40*) For example, the local gypsies used to come to our door selling pegs, etc. – and did so with such regularity that Mum designated separate mugs for each of them. Once, whilst sipping their brew on the doorstep, one of the gypsies admired my mum's 'pinny' (one of those full-length coveralls with a bib and cross straps at the back). She didn't hesitate in her obedience to the Lord's command by taking it straight off and giving it to her.

> *Mum had the same generosity, living by the Bible truth that, "if any man will sue thee, and take away thy coat, let him have thy cloak also."*

Dad, though, was always eager for ways to spread the word in a larger way. As he himself would say, rather elegantly "One aspect of my desire is to display the word of God". His spark for bold statements was ignited during a holiday to the north Welsh coast. Dad climbed to the summit of the Great Orme, a limestone headland famous for having Britain's only cable tram car. At the summit, he looked down into the abyss of rock and sea below. There, painted on the rocks at the bottom and looking right back up to the top of the Orme, were the words 'Jesus Saves'. The message came as such an unexpected surprise that it made a deep impression on Dad and stimulated him thereafter to look for ways to erect 'big' signs for Jesus himself.

In fact, he got cracking the very next time there was a family outing to Scarborough. Dad loved building enormous sandcastles. He has built hundreds for children over the years, and the fine, golden sands of Scarborough's beaches are perfect for this activity. Dad' craft was such that his castles would always feature turrets and bridges, with a huge moat surrounding his creation. Heavy lifting complete, on this occasion, he left the kids to fill the moat with water and decorate the turrets with shells while he pootled off to the north side of the town where there is a high point overlooking the beach He'd had a big idea – and proceeded to spend a long hour drawing enormous letters to form 'Jesus Saves' in the sand with his foot.

There was always another opportunity to spread the Gospel, and Dad particularly looked forward to the next Easter celebration, as he had had another idea for broadcasting the word of God. Pressing his trusty company Ford Cortina into service of the Lord, he used the top of two trestle tables to construct a billboard sign for the roof of the car. Utilising the signwriting skills he had acquired in the course of his work, he painted each side of the table beautifully with the Bible text, *Christ, the Lord hath risen*, then lashed the two tables together with rope to form a sturdy triangle - or 'A board' – to be hoisted onto the roof rack. As the finishing touch, Dad mounted his tannoy speaker

Dare to be a Daniel

on the roof and threaded the mouthpiece through the window on the driver's side.

On Easter Sunday morning, the family pressed into the car in their Sunday best (including obligatory hats for the ladies)- as Dad drove along, proclaiming the joyful message aloft. Whenever Dad saw someone on the pavement, he would direct a personal message of joy to them from his speaker. A comical, campaigning charabanc for God. Inside the car, however, Mum and my sister maintained stoic faces throughout, while I personally died a thousand deaths for fear someone from my school might see me! Dad himself was very happy with his campaign, and between services that day, he continued to drive around the community broadcasting the good news – alone!

> *Unfortunately, Dad sometimes got a little too carried away with his enthusiasm. In his most ambitious attempt to prominently display the word of God, he set his sights on the top of Cheddar Gorge*

Unfortunately, Dad sometimes got a little too carried away with his enthusiasm. In his most ambitious attempt to prominently display the word of God, he set his sights on the top of Cheddar Gorge during a family camping holiday in Somerset. Gazing up to the top of the Gorge 400 ft away, he thought how wonderful it would be for unbelievers to see God's word on the top. And so that evening, fired by his evangelical zeal, he called in at the hardware shop and bought a pot of white emulsion. He then proceeded to carry it all the way to the top of the Gorge and got to work.

Satisfied, he drove the family out the next morning to show off his handiwork; the massive lettering of 'Jesus Saves' written out along the top of the gorge, not unlike the famous Hollywood billboard in California. The elation invoked by the prominent display of God's word was cut short, however, by the small but firm voice of my mother, suggesting that the letters might be defiling a magnificent natural and national monument of a rather more permanent nature than the shifting sand of Scarborough beach. This evoked a sudden crisis of conscience, resulting in Dad promptly rescaling the precipitous summit at the top of the Gorge, this time armed with water and a scrubbing brush to erase the offending letters.

I often wonder whether anyone passed through the Gorge on that day, perhaps seeking answers to life's questions after a depressing day at work; looked up and saw what he thought was a spiritual message directed personally to him - like the hand that wrote the message at *Belshazzar's Feast* - and for his resolve to harden the next morning to find the words had disappeared overnight!

Our family holidays were invariably spent camping or caravanning. Before the start of any of these long excursions, the family would kneel together on the lounge floor and pray for God's hand of protection on the journey. This was almost definitely a result of one particularly disturbing occasion, trying to get my sister,

Christine, home from teaching college in Manchester, a few hours' drive across the Pennines. Dad had accepted a lift from a man in the Assembly who owned a car – only to find it was a three-wheeler! Shortly after setting off towards home carrying four people in it (for some reason, they had offered a lift to another student), the car turned too sharply on a bend, overturned, and rolled down a steep bank. Miraculously no one was harmed, but several hours later, their rescue car – an Austin A30 driven by Grandpa Alf – suffered a catastrophic burst tyre on the notorious Pennine Snake Pass, spinning out of control and stopping just short of a vertiginous drop by the side of the road. Hence the pre-journey prayer ritual - and the packing of a flask of hot, strong tea (tea bags left inside) – began.

While on holiday, Dad would seek out the local Gospel Hall, turning up on a Sunday morning - being, to my eternal dismay, the very first day of our holiday - with a letter of commendation from our home Assembly, assuring them we were 'in fellowship'. We would, without question, be given a warm welcome and, more often than not, invited home by complete strangers for Sunday dinner. It never failed to amaze me that having a common faith usually ensured a nice time would be had by all. Some of these people even became my parents' lifelong friends.

During one caravan holiday in Somerset, when we were not within reasonable reach of Gospel Hall, Dad decided to hold a Sunday School for the campsite children in the caravan – going around the site on Sunday morning with a personal invite to each child. Some of the parents took up the invitation, and it wasn't long before sounds of enthusiastic chorus-singing and story-telling echoed around the campsite. I wonder whether any of those children, now in their fifties, still recall this unique caravan church service.

Some Summers our family spent an entire week on a beach spreading the good news of Jesus. We volunteered with the United Beach Mission who organised summer open-air meetings for children at British seaside resorts. The Noons most frequently went to Bridlington where we would sleep on the floor of a Methodist Church which had a prominent position on the sea front. Mum was designated cook to a large team of volunteers. Dad and I donned our bright red beach mission t-shirt with enthusiasm to join in games, singing and prayers, 4 times a day on the beach.

Dad's boundless, childlike enthusiasm made it great fun to have Denis as our Dad. At our birthday parties, we couldn't wait for him to come home from work so he could join us in our games. He was the Dad who, on Bonfire night, didn't mind if we tied firecrackers to his belt to make him leap comically around. When it snowed, he would be the first to suggest gathering up the other kids in the street to climb to the top of the hill in Pontefract Park and slide down on plastic sacks. He is equally fearless, too. He once bought a small boat, named it Daniel, and joined a sailing club, so we could all learn to sail. Not satisfied with the calmness of the club lake however, Dad took me and the tiny boat down the enormous river Beale, on a windy day. Shortly after setting sail, the wind broke our mast in two! We were miles from anywhere with few options - but I didn't imagine that one of them would be for Dad to stand on the bow and hold up the mast long enough to get us to the nearest civilisation!

Yet there were small compromises we children had to make as a result of our parents' firm beliefs. For example, us girls weren't allowed to wear trousers, as the Scripture states that men and women should dress distinctly. That said, I do remember winning the arguing that I should be allowed to wear trousers on my forthcoming potholing school trip. To my amazement, I was allowed to have them.... as long as I wore a dress on top! Dad once tore up my sister Ruth's blasphemous record cover for *Godspell,* as it showed a man who played Jesus wearing a badge that said, 'I am Jesus Christ'. My eldest sister Christine was disappointed she couldn't go on the Working Men's Club seaside outing with her friend Kathleen, while my brother Robert would never work with Dad as he never had the right tools for any job, being reluctant to waste money on none-but-essential items! The family rarely watched TV as so much of the content was ungodly. The range of programs we were permitted to watch was confined to the News, The Waltons, Little House on the Prairie, and University Challenge. Surprisingly, given how little TV Dad consumed, Dad became a fan of 'Detective Columbo'. However, I'll admit I shared Dad's disappointment to learn that Columbo had succumbed to visiting a nightclub in the course of his investigations, and this unedifying behaviour forced Dad to get rid of his DVD box set.

Dare to be a Daniel

In hindsight, all of our childhood compromises and disquiets at the time have turned into nothing more than amusing anecdotes. Dad and Mum's faith set a gold standard parenting template. Walking in Christ's footsteps made them consistently contented. Mum and Dad never complained, swore, or shared their worries, and were unswerving in their drive to do the right thing. Our suburban world spread surprisingly far due to the huge network of Assembly people and their outreach activities. The childhood of us four children was full, nurtured, and surprisingly laid back, as the Lord shared a hand in our welfare as well as our parents. In our house, there was laughter, drama, music, warmth, and always possibilities. We could say with certainty that our sweet tins were always full of Angel cake.

Dare to be a Daniel

Beach Mission 1960s.

Family camping holiday in Scotland, 1970s.with the current Ford Cortina complete with homemade roof rack (L-R Christine, Ruth, Jenny & Denis)

Dare to be a Daniel

Denis with a stack of Bibles.

Chapter 17: Defending the Faith

No enemy is too big when you've fought the devil and won, and Dad's second worst enemy was the Catholic faith, or 'Rome' as Dad refers to it.

In 1982, Pope John Paul II planned a visit to the north of England - the first visit to the UK by a reigning Pope and said to be the biggest event for UK Catholics since their emancipation. It should be noted that the north of England wasn't the Pope's first choice. He'd planned to visit Northern Ireland, where there were far more Catholics receptive to his visit. However, fiery Ian Paisley, leader of the Free Presbyterian Church of Ulster (of whom Dad was a BIG fan), had made it clear that John Paul wasn't welcome and had threatened protests if John Paul ventured even close to the Stranraer ferry. So, it came to be that the Pope limited his UK tour to England, Scotland and Wales.

On one particular day, a mass was planned to be held on the York racecourse. For a venue of this size they were obviously expecting quite a crowd. Dad and the Assembly had the same anti- 'Rome' reasons as Mr. Paisley for objecting to the Pope's presence in their backyard; the reason being that Catholicism rejects 'justification by faith'. In other words, it is only by faith that you are saved from sin - and not through anything that you can do yourself. 'Rome' had introduced the words that "partly by works," he is saved, which, in Dad's view, opened the door to earning your salvation through good works - quite contrary to the teaching of the Scriptures. Dad's firm view is that Catholics think they can intercede between man and God and impose tithes and penances to influence their destination in the after-life. But Dad saw eye-to-eye with Martin Luther on this point, that humans are saved through faith alone (sola fide), and therefore someone needed to show the Pope that his views were wrong. Since Martin Luther wasn't around to do anything about it, and ignoring the fact that here had been an assassination attempt on the Pope's life less than a month previously, Dad started to plan:

> *I planned to sit on the ladder and preach the gospel when the Pope started speaking. . . . I spent a good deal of time in the back garden painting a banner made from rolls of wallpaper*

"On the York racecourse, there is a grandstand which is where I assumed the Pope would be speaking from. I drove there (about a 40-mile round trip) to investigate. To my delight, I found that at the rear of the stand, there was a flat-roofed area, only one storey high, 15 ft or so from the ground. I saw that a ladder with a hook on the end would be capable of being hooked onto the lower roof and I could climb up. I planned to go early in the morning and hide there until the appropriate time. I would then pull up the ladder and use it to climb onto the hip of the higher-sloping roof. There, I would be behind the

Dare to be a Daniel

podium and I could perch on the ladder, unfurl a banner and preach the gospel when the Pope started speaking.

I would use the portable loudspeaker that we used in open-air work at times. We didn't always amplify our preaching as it sometimes caused irritation - i.e., people would complain with shouts of 'clear off'! - and so a lot of the time, we relied on the fact that if you lift up your voice and shout and sing as loud as is humanly possible (without blacking out and fainting) and make a cheerful noise to the Lord, this would be good enough. Since there was no musical accompaniment, the first note of the hymns would have to be 'struck up', usually by me. Occasionally I would get the pitch wrong, but once you've started, there is no going back, and if, in the course of one of these mistakes, there came along a note too high to reach, we would valiantly aim for it, however red and breathless it left us after several verses.

I had a hook made specially by a blacksmith in Castleford, which I screwed onto the top of the ladder. I spent a good deal of time in the back garden painting a banner made from rolls of wallpaper – which, thanks to my line of work, there was always a ready supply. The banner simply stated the words: 'Justification by Faith'. I had a car that could carry a ladder on the roof rack and, on the appointed day, when it was dusk, I set off. I had sussed out a spot at the side of the racecourse where I could park my car and walk to the building. I had my loudspeaker slung over one shoulder and my ladder over the other. However, when I got a close distance to the building, I saw, to my dismay, that it was surrounded by hordes of security people and stewards who looked as if they had been there all night. It would have been impossible for me to have got any closer without being seen. returned home, accepting that it was the mind of the Lord that it ought not to be. It was going too far."

Family holidays continued to provide opportunities for witnessing however and the relocation of my sister Christine 'down South proffered the tantalising prospect of lifting the veil of unbelief from the people of the UK's most populous city. This move also brought joy to my mother, my sister Ruth, and me, as our visits brought us within reach of the Royal Family, who we loved. We would frequently coincide a visit to 'our Christine's' with a royal event – even something as low-key as the annual opening of parliament; we were delighted with the pomp and parade and passing glimpse of a familiar royal face.

To make it to London in time to witness these events, we would excitedly get up at the crack of dawn and drive the 10 miles from Enfield into the centre of London, parking by the river off Lower Thames Street. Through many similar excursions, we had found we could discreetly park between the abandoned warehouses right on the riverfront, so as to avoid any parking fees. This even turned out to be the perfect Royal-watching spot on one occasion. We had heard that the Queen was to come up the Thames on a boat as part of her Jubilee celebration, and we shouted and waved furiously as she passed - she saw us and waved right back!

Dare to be a Daniel

We didn't always have the best view from the roadside, but Dad would put his enterprise to the best possible use on every occasion to get us to see the parade. On the day of the Silver Jubilee service in 1977, where the Queen was expected at St Paul's Cathedral, we arrived to find crowds reaching 10ft deep.

There would be no chance of finding a spot to see the Queen. But Dad being Dad, noticed a 12ft wall behind him (I've been back to measure it!), found a building site around the corner, and, inside, located a ladder. He was fearless with ladders and had no qualms about borrowing it either, as it was a Saturday and the builders wouldn't need it. He propped the ladder against the wall, and we all scuttled up to sit on the wall. A birds-eye view and, the envy of the crowd, and it wasn't long before some American ladies spoke to us, and Dad, of course, invited them up to join us. He nipped down the ladder and escorted them all to the top (to their *'oohs*, *'aahs*, and shrieks of delight). We shuffled along to accommodate them and ended up with an uninterrupted view of the Queen on the steps of St Paul's, wearing her bright pink coat and a distinctive spray of bells on her matching hat. After the fun of getting down the ladder was over, the ladder was duly returned to the building site, of course.

On these week-long holidays spent with our Christine, it became a habit of Dad's to spend the Wednesday in London on his own, in order to spread the Gospel. Initially, he would go to Speakers' Corner in Hyde Park, which had a ready-made crowd with a listening ear. He would patiently wait his turn and then step up onto a milk crate to preach the word of God. Sometimes he would just choose a busy corner to start preaching or handing out tracts to help open a spiritual conversation with a stranger - a less aggressive version of today's charity chuggers. Tracts are small paper leaflets containing a Gospel message, and the cover features an arresting soul-searching question such as: 'Where will you spend eternity?', 'Does God exist?', or, more curiously, 'Is it sinful to be a soldier?'

But Dad wasn't alone in his unwavering obedience to the commandment to spread the word of God. "On one of these Wednesdays, I was wandering past the Tower of London, and I heard preaching in the gardens there," he recalls. "I spoke to the fella, and it turns out his name was Bill, and he worked in a solicitor's office nearby. During his lunch hour every day, he would stand and preach at Tower Hill, where there were plenty of tourists. I knew that if I went there at that time, he would be there. Others would join him too, and his dedication would be the inspiration when I got back home, to do our own open-air work in Airedale. A group of adults would walk to a spot in Airedale and have an open-air meeting. We would sing and preach hoping we would draw a crowd."

Dad fell in with Bill unconditionally. He accompanied him at his Wednesday lunchtime preaching slot for over thirty years, never learning anything more about him - not so much as his phone number. "It was sufficient to know that we shared the same religious beliefs. However, one day, I went to the usual spot in the gardens opposite the Tower of London, and Bill wasn't there. One of his 'regular' listeners

Dare to be a Daniel

told me that he had passed away. I was shattered, and it ended the episode of that particular outreach endeavour."

Supporting missionaries who have ventured overseas to spread God's word has been at the heart of Dad's spiritual life. The calendar highlight for this was the missionary conference held annually in a large church in Leeds. Missionaries would be invited there to talk about their work. They represented a vast range of countries for, as we are constantly reminded, there are sinners everywhere. But the missionaries I remember most were those based in culturally remote countries like Chad, Brazil, Cameroon, and the jungles of the Congo.

Talks from these missionaries were compelling travel stories with a twist for three reasons. First, these missionaries had responded to a 'calling' when they chose their destination. To be 'called' implied there was hard work to be done, which meant they wouldn't be welcomed with open arms. The opposite, in fact, they would be distinctly unwelcome, from a religious point of view as they were there to persuade the locals to change their religious beliefs. Secondly - and most extraordinarily - they went 'in faith', which meant they had no money. They completely relied on funding from their local church or from readers of the missionary in-house magazine *Echoes of Service*. Thirdly, these people always took their families with them on this perilous venture. Talk about brave!

Given this jeopardy, it's not surprising that their reports were exciting. We measured their success on how many people they had brought to salvation and the colourful ways the Lord had managed to provide them with food and shelter. No missionary ever admitted to coming home through lack of money, nor was any of them hacked to death by fierce natives, so I have to conclude the faith method must work.

Dad has sent funds to missionaries all his life. The pinboard in his kitchen features a Missionary Map with pictures of these brave people exhorting us to continue to pray for them and send funds.

In the '70s and '80s, before the walls of communism crumbled missionaries weren't permitted in these countries, and so smuggling Bibles where Christian practice was illegal was one of the only ways to conduct missionary activities. A Dutch Christian Missionary called Brother Andrew, known as 'God's Smuggler', used to slip past border guards in his blue VW Beetle with Bibles on his front seat in plain sight, praying, "Lord, when you walked this earth, you made blind eyes see. Now I pray, make seeing eyes blind!". His direct approach worked - and he became a figurehead for the charity Open Doors which pulled off the most exciting Bible smuggling feat ever in 1981.

One night, twenty brave Christians successfully sailed a container ship to China in secret and unloaded a million Bibles onto the beach. These Bibles, it's said, were a pivotal moment in helping to replace the millions burned in Mao's Cultural Revolution.

It was one thing to send money towards the Bible-smuggling cause, but another entirely to actually participate in it. One day, our family came home to find the hallway stacked high with boxes of

Bibles. This was not unusual in itself, as Dad was a Gideon and gave Bibles and new testaments out at school assemblies and to hotels. However, these Bibles were all written in Chinese! Dad was cagey about what his role was in the process, but it did cross our minds that smuggling carried a prison sentence in some countries. To our relief, though, Dad was merely a 'middleman' and promptly passed his contraband onto someone else later in the week. Poskitt's van was no doubt used to aid and abet the operation.

Chapter 18: The End of the Line.

So, what became of the railway carriage home? Denis takes up the story again.

"I moved out when we got married, living at first with Lois's Dad, stepmum, and stepbrother Donald in Ashton Road, he recalls. Our visits to the railway carriage were usually to walk over there to have dinner with the family. I would often go to see my parents on my own on my bike.

My brother Peter moved into the Hoof's house after they died, and he brought up his three boys there with his wife, Margaret. He had a well for water but no electricity and so they eventually went to live in Featherstone. As the years rolled by, the council would write to us to say that the spring contained surface drainage water and wasn't up to the safety standard required – though the water never did us any harm. However,

Mam and Dad eventually wanted things to be a bit easier, and in 1953, when I was twenty-five and Dad was sixty-seven years old, Dad and Mam moved out of the railway carriage into a little council house close by in Whitwood Mere. They had lived in the railway carriage in Carr Wood for 31 years. I remember that the Queen had just had her Coronation, and Edmund Hilary and Tenzing Norgay had just conquered Everest. Britain was still recovering from World War Two, and rationing was still in place.

At this point, having no means of income from the farm, my brother Danny went to Australia. He emigrated as a 'Ten Pound Pom' as part of their novel 'Populate or Perish' scheme, designed to provide a workforce for their booming industries. Danny, however, could only find work as a window cleaner in Perth. However, Having consistently resisted the family's faith, he finally found his way to the Gospel Hall and was converted.

In 1965, we were sent word that he had contracted bowel cancer, and it was a shock to find out how ill he was. We knew we couldn't get to Australia in time to see him before he died. Commercial flights to Australia didn't commence until the 1970s, and it would take six weeks to sail to Perth. But Dad felt he wanted to go over for the funeral and asked me to go with him. We discussed with the family how we might club together to pay for Dad and me to go, but it was judged by all to be too far away for the money involved and not worth it.

John continued to live on his own there for a while, farming the land, but even he eventually succumbed to the lure of running water and electricity and moved into a house in Cutsyke, near the Gospel Hall. He went to live in Bradford later on with his wife Anne, whom he had met after learning to dance.

I am the only one left of 'Noonies' ten thousand kids. I remained close to all of my brothers and sisters throughout their lives through our shared love of nature and walking, especially in the Yorkshire countryside. For decades, we would meet up with them and their families at a designated spot for a pre-planned circular walk. Lady

Dare to be a Daniel

Bower Damn in the Peak District and Simon's Seat in the Yorkshire Dales were favourite spots.

Eventually, my parents were taken in to be cared for by Freda and Ernest until they were taken on as housekeepers at Castle Howard. Then Jessie and her trumpet-playing husband, Joe, took them into their house on the Westfield Estate, where she was a community warden for retired people. It was whilst he was being cared for by Jessie that Dad died in tragic circumstances.

At the Saturday night meeting at North Featherstone Gospel Hall we were told that Dad had gone missing after going for a walk. It was summertime. Jessie said he had gone walking towards Noonies at her suggestion. Since Dad had developed Alzheimer's, the police had been in the habit of bringing him home whenever he went missing. This time, a party of people went over to Noonies to look for him. A lot of people got to know that he was missing and joined us. Many were out all night looking for him, including me.

On Sunday morning, we resumed the search. One man said, 'Most of you have been along the paths, I'm going to walk along the railway', and as he did, he had a clear view of the muck stack adjacent to Noonies. He spied a pile of old clothes which suddenly moved, and he realised he had found him; Dad had slipped into a gulley and couldn't move, having caught his foot in a piece of wire. He was trapped and had had to stay there all night – and in the rain, too. It will always be to my sorrow that I had been walking on the top of the muck stack and didn't go to where he had dropped down to the railway. H was taken to Pontefract General Infirmary but died at home a couple of weeks later."

Chapter 19: Denis Retires

Like his father, Daniel, Dad has inherited a powerful work ethic as he explains below.

"After my retirement, aged sixty-five, I was walking past the old firm (Poskitt Pallets) when I saw piles of pallets in their forecourt. This was a bad sign as it meant that pallet sales were down. I went inside and had a chat with Brenda, their accountant. She said they couldn't afford a salesperson. I replied that I would be their salesperson and wouldn't charge them a penny. For the next few years, I secured a number of good orders by spotting companies using pallets and asking what they were paying for them. I was often able to undercut them and make a sale. The fire to help others in need continues to burn. Time in retirement provides me with the chance to help others in need, especially if it also furthers the Lord's work."

Dad's painting skills came in handy when answering a call for help to refurbish a hostel for the homeless in Dublin. He spent weeks at a time there with his friend Ron Cosgrove, sleeping on the floor whilst he painted and decorated during the day.

Being a devoted cyclist, he was also quick to answer an appeal for bicycles to send to Africa. Through word of mouth and a small note in the chip shop, he managed to collect twenty bicycles. Some of them were lost/stolen bikes donated by the police. Everyone was very

Dare to be a Daniel

generous. The kind bike repairer, for example, who donated twenty repair kits and pumps.

Eventually, someone delivered the bikes to Manchester, where Dad's precious collection was locked in a container ready for onward shipping to Africa. Regretfully, they didn't make it *any* further. That same night, the container was broken into, and all the bikes were stolen.

Yet despite occasional setbacks over the years, Dad's drive to spread the precious word has not diminished, and, in his eighties, Dad came up with one of his best evangelising schemes yet - the 'Motorway Text' project. For a long time, Dad had seen value in the large audiences that moved along the local M62 and A1 each day. Taking his opportunity, he built a removable apex sign displaying a Bible text to put on top of his car. He would then take the sign, drive off the A1 left-hand carriageway, park at an angle to the oncoming traffic and mount his sign on the roof of the car. Another favourite spot was to park on top of a motorway bridge. He would sit and read the Bible while he waited for the word of the scripture to work its way into the hearts of the Northbound motorists.

One day though, as he drove to one of his usual spots, it occurred to him that he could reach more people by having a permanent sign on the side of the road. He had already noticed how lorry trailers in farmers' fields could be used to display advertising. And so, upon spotting four empty lorry trailers, his local knowledge came into full force as he tracked down the farmers who owned them. The trailers were on the busy intersection of the A1 and the M62, very close to Noonies' fields, in fact. He negotiated a rental fee with each farmer then had large red vinyl letters made up after consulting with various people on which colours have the most visual impact. Whilst waiting for the letters to arrive, he cleaned and painted the trailers white to ensure a good contrast with the letters. In the meantime, a helpful member of the congregation also made him a web page that pointed people to the local Gospel Hall and to Dad's address for free Gospel literature.

Assemblies far and wide saw and heard about the Motorway Text venture and began offering financial support. Undoubtedly, the most impactful trailer was the one situated at Barnsdale Bar, close to junction 25 on the A1. The poor road layout at this point means the traffic is usually proceeding at a slow crawl, providing all motorist with plenty of time to reflect on the prescient message, 'Prepare to meet your God'. This sign looks particularly dramatic at certain time of the year, when it is surrounded by snow or when the rapeseed is in glorious flower.

Dad kept the Motorway Text signs going long after his failing eyesight prevented him from driving to the signs for maintenance. Undeterred, he would catch the bus carrying a stiff broom and in his haversack a flask of hot water and a handsaw to cut back the bramble. He'd use the hot water and broom to wash the letters clean.

Eventually, after fourteen years of dedicated cleaning and pruning the removal of some Brexit graffiti, and around £100,000 in donations, Dad was approached by a Christian couple in Scotland who organise similar signs across the UK, Africa and Canada called 'Hope by the Roadside' (https://www.hopebytheroadside.com). They offered to take on the Motorway Text responsibility, and Dad readily accepted - it is a joy for him to know that his outreach venture will continue.

The Bible imposes a strict obligation for Christians to obey the law of the land, but it also exhorts Christians to separate God's work from the law. This principle is illustrated in the verse: "Render therefore unto Caesar the things which are Caesar's, and unto God the things that are God's." The family always regarded this as quite a shame because Dad has a wide knowledge and takes a close interest in world politics (especially anything to do with Israel, for obvious reasons), and his daily routine includes reading a daily newspaper, listening to Radio 4's *World at One* and watching the weekly highlights of *Question Time* and *Prime Minister's Question Time*. His beliefs, however, prevent him from exercising his right to vote. Yet Dad is grateful that the British constitution has allowed him to practice his faith unimpeded – that is, until the outbreak of Covid-19.

Dad, of course, complied with lockdown rules but viewed the requirement to isolate as far from ideal, as it denied Christians the fellowship of other Christians. Dad and Mum effortlessly conducted their meetings, just the two of them at home throughout the Lockdown period. This included enacting the Breaking of Bread service in their front room. They were as faithful as they could be to perform the ritual as it would usually be performed in the Gospel Hall. They held it at the usual time on Sunday morning, dressed appropriately - Dad in his best shirt, tie and suit; Mum in an obligatory head covering in the form of a brimmed hat - and laid out on a small table the emblems of unleavened bread (Matzo crackers), representing Christ's body, and the wine (cup of squash), representing Christ's blood. Those in fellowship are expected to give, and they also remembered to pass around the offering plate, just between the two of them! I guess Dad rather dominated these meetings, whilst they don't have a set form, only men are allowed to contribute with a prayer or scripture, or to give a Christ-centred thought. Mum's role is limited to giving out the hymns and joining in the singing!

Covid-19's lockdown rules did skirt dangerously close to inhibiting Dad's free religious practice, and Dad scrutinised the lockdown rules with as much fervour as if he were defending his religious rights against a secular state. There were two recommendations he particularly found an issue with. Firstly, he stubbornly subverted the 'no singing in church' rule by humming behind his mask. But what he objected to more than anything was the idea of not being able to share the blood of Christ by everyone drinking from the same communion cup. After much scrutiny of the Government's wording, the congregation conceded to offer a tray of small wine-filled glasses, poured from the communal cup *and* the communion cup itself for the diehards, should anyone choose to flirt

Dare to be a Daniel

with the virus. I don't even have to ask to know which option Dad chose.

The Airedale Sunday School ran for more than 50 years with a dedicated group of fellow workers, including wonderful people like Pat Webster and Gloria Dale. The Airedale Assembly meetings soldier on, although numbers have declined dramatically. Brethren Assemblies with more progressive approaches have thrived, the Cutsyke Assembly being one of them. The more conservative assemblies, such as the Castleford Assembly founded by Daniel and Maud Noon, closed their doors in 2021. This was a short-lived blessing for Airedale Assembly, as they took on some of its remaining congregation. Importantly, this influx doubled the male members of the congregation to four – crucial, since only men can lead meetings - giving hope to prolong the life of the Airedale Assembly.

Sadly, though, this hope was short-lived. In one dreadful week in January 2022, both these 'brothers' passed away, along with my mother, Lois. There are now only two remaining male members of the congregation, and one of those is 'incentivised' to attend the service.

After 75 years, Dad's doctrinal beliefs remain unchanged, and his love of Christ undiminished. It's not an exaggeration to say that every one of his waking thoughts and actions is still imbued with how to glorify the Lord.

Unlike Daniel, Dad hasn't ever been tested by being thrown into a lion's den, but nonetheless he has been unerringly obedient in his

Dare to be a Daniel

service to Jesus Christ. He has unquestionably 'Dared to be a Daniel, dared to stand alone, dared to have a purpose true and dared to make it know.' In later life, when questioned, he expresses surprise about his fortitude and ability to stand alone. He asserts it "wasn't inherent at all. It was a gift bestowed on me at the point of salvation".

Dad continues to take a banner bearing bible texts, on the bus to Castleford or Pontefract town centre on Saturday afternoons to use to preach to the shoppers. He is frequently recognised by locals who talk to him of fondly remembered outings, prizes, skating, walks, and sunshine corners.

And despite his increasingly failing eyesight, he still rides his bike and has just used it to complete the posting of 3,000 Gospel tracts into local homes. Above all, he continues to 'Dare to be a Daniel' - and was last seen on the roof of the Gospel Hall, looking for a persistent leak over the organ.

Dare to be a Daniel

Walking with Peter around Ladybower Dam.

Dare to be a Daniel

The Motorway Text trailer at Barnsdale Bar.

Chapter 20: The Last Stop

It's not surprising that it was an act of kindness that drew Dad back to the place of his birth. He recalls:

"I did go back to the railway carriage once. I used to visit an old lady in Glasshoughton, and she mentioned that she loved Pussy Willows. I knew there would be some at Noonies, and I remember walking along the path from the farm buildings to the carriage. All was desolate and overgrown, and it was clear that it was unused. I tried the door handle of the old railway carriage, and the door swung open. The windows had been broken. There were bits of furniture strewn around. The old fireplace, where we used to get as near to it as we could to get warm, was still there, and all was still. It was as if the place was held together with memories.

Suddenly something moved. Shocked, I turned to see some remnants of lace curtain wafting in the breeze from the broken window. The Bible talks about Eli's daughter, who gave birth after she was told that Israel had lost the battle with the Philistines who had captured the ark of the covenant. The baby survived, and they named him Ichabod – which means 'the glory has departed'. This is what I thought of when I saw the curtain move. I used this in future sermons to illustrate that when people 'backslid' from the Assembly, the glory had departed from them. The glory had certainly departed from Noonies' railway carriage. I have carried on visiting the site for the cooking apples which grow from five apple trees that Dad planted.

Dare to be a Daniel

Eventually and predictably, vandals burned the carriage down, but the site of the railway carriage remains untouched. Nature took over long ago, but remarkably, the bricks that formed the foundations of the lower story remained until 2021."

Since Daniel and Maud left their homestead, the small green fields around Carr Wood have witnessed massive change to their surroundings. In 1960, the M62 sliced through the countryside on its way to Manchester and largely cut off access to Pontefract. The closure of Glasshoughton Colliery in 1986 became the site where they built the entertainment magnet, Junction 32, and the muck stack on the other side of the beck has been levelled to provide space for an estate of new houses. On the hedge side, adjacent to the spring, a further estate of houses encroaches, whose streets are named after race courses, presumably in homage to the one they would have a view of if they could see past the M62.

The smell of the coke ovens has been replaced with the whiff of engines from the motorway, and the traffic noise has replaced the thrum of the coal buckets on the muck stack. Dad has no regrets, as he agrees with others of his generation – that all these developments represent progress.

The soft footprint of Daniel and Maud's home still remains however. The site of Carr Wood itself is now close to being sold and it seems fitting that exactly 100 years since the last 'eco' house left its gentle footprint, there are now plans to site four houses with the highest eco standards. I wonder if the new occupants will ever know that this piece of land once provided a home to a young Christian family who lived in a converted railway carriage they had sited there a hundred years ago.

Daniel Noon, a courageous former miner, realised a dream to raise his family on a smallholding. He and his wife Maud drew water from a spring, created warmth from burning wood, ate vegetables and fruit from their own crops and apple trees, and kept their own livestock. You can't get much more eco than that!

Dare to be a Daniel

Denis and Lois still smiling after 73 years of marriage.

Dare to be a Daniel

Acknowledgements

I would like to thank all the people who have been so generous with their time and spirit to help me complete this book. Special thanks go to my dear friend David Allsop, whose editing skills, cajoling, and enthusiasm gave me the boost to finish this story to a much higher standard than I could ever have hoped for.

I would also like to thank my esteemed former colleague Paul Phillips and his daughter Hannah whose astute sub-editing of the story was no small task.

Grateful thanks go to Nick Hirst, whose illustration of Carr Wood was so beautifully imagined using only an old OS map and a shakily drawn plan by my father. Check out his fabulous work at https://www.pinterest.co.uk/nickhirstlondon/

I also want to give huge thanks to Gabriella Stratis, my friend's daughter, a talented art student. She enthusiastically and painstakingly produced a wonderful illustration of the railway carriage interior and Noon family tree.

I would also like to especially thank my lovely niece Ellie Palmer for her expertise in designing the book covers.

Permission to insert the photograph of Prepare to Meet your God was generously granted by photographer Stephen Fareham at www.geograph.org.uk.

Printed in Great Britain
by Amazon